D.J.Dodds
June 1992

New Flowers

New Flowers

GROWING THE NEW GARDEN VARIETIES

TESSA PAUL

CONSULTANT EDITOR, DAPHNE LEDWARD

HARRY N. ABRAMS, INC., PUBLISHERS, NEW YORK

Library of Congress Cataloging-in-Publication Data
Paul, Tessa.
New flowers: growing the new garden varieties / Tessa Paul:
consultant editor, Daphne Ledward.
p.   cm.
ISBN 0–8109–3651–8
1. Flowers. 2. Flowers—Varieties. 3. Flowers—Pictorial works.
4. Flowers—Varieties—Pictorial works.   I. Ledward. Daphne.
II. Title.
SB407.P373   1990
635.9—dc20   90–32715

Published in 1990 by Harry N. Abrams, Incorporated,
New York
A Times Mirror Company

New Flowers is a Marshall Edition
Editor: Ruth Binney
Art Director: John Bigg
Principal Photographer: Andrew Lawson

Printed and bound in Belgium

Photographs: 1/ *Fuchsia* 'Leonora'; 2/ clockwise from top left *Trillium erectum*,
Rose 'English Heritage', *Euphorbia marginata* 'Berg Kristall', *Aquilegia* 'Nora
Barlow'; 3/ *Primula auricula* 'Stubb's Tartan'; 4/ *Celosia cristata* 'Olympia Mixed';
5/ *Gazania* 'Sutton's Hybrids'

CONTENTS

INTRODUCTION

The quest for new flowers is not a twentieth-century phenomenon. The great plant hunters of the past brought us the forerunners of many of the flowers we now take for granted, and which have so widened the choice available.

Plant discovery is a continuing process, but new plants suited to temperate climates do not necessarily demand intrepid exploits. They can appear as a result of natural cross-breeding or spontaneous mutation ("sporting") in situations no more exotic than the average suburban garden.

The ability to "sport" – to produce flowers, foliage, or other parts distinctly different from the main plant – is extremely pronounced in certain

ZINNIA 'STATE FAIR MIXED' BEING RAISED IN MASSED BEDS TO test for garden potential.

genera, species (subgroups within a genus with similar traits), or varieties (specific types of plants within a species). Some roses, fuchsias, dahlias, and pelargoniums, for example, mutate freely.

The plant breeder can propagate, from cuttings taken from the mutated plant or part of the plant, any sport that shows signs of being a promising new variety. If the sport proves stable and does not revert to the original after growing on, usually for more than three years, it can then be put into commercial production. It is essential to allow sufficient time for such trialing, since many sports revert in the first or second generation after they first occur. Sporting can be induced in some plants by irradiation, a controversial technique that is sometimes used on chrysanthemums.

However, the majority of the plant breeders' work concerns the crossing of species or varieties. This mixes their genes (the "factors" in the cells that code for the individual's characteristics) to produce new cultivars, that is, varieties produced in cultivation

*A DAHLIA GROWING AT A TRIAL GROUND. IT IS NOT YET
sufficiently established to be named.*

The fact that human nature makes us yearn for the unattainable explains the great effort poured into the search for the blue rose, orange fuchsia, black tulip, and the like. In such quests, the breeder looks for parents appearing to carry a particular colour gene and with skillful hybridization, usually over many years, the goal comes ever nearer. It will remain a matter of dispute as to whether the resultant color break is really worth all the effort, but the challenge is always there. There is some way to go before we see the true blue rose – those currently marketed as "blue" are more like a muddy lilac – but the breeders' dream of the true red delphinium became a reality in the late 1980s.

Hybridization can be used to breed in good characteristics, or breed out bad ones. It has created bush roses that flower more or less perpetually throughout the summer, not just in early or later flushes, and varieties of crocosmia that do not have invasive habits. And we now have new cultivars of potentially over-large shrubs such as choisya and weigela which are compact enough to be acceptable in a small garden.

All new varieties are rigorously trialed for several years until the breeders are sure they are worthy of universal introduction. During this time they are given no special treatment other than the general requirements of the particular type of plant under

*POPPIES ARE AMONG THE OLD-FASHIONED FLOWERS NOW BEING
newly hybridized for garden use.*

rather than in the wild. Apart from the novelty factor of producing something that looks different, hybridization is often beneficial, since it can result in a boost to vigor and general well-being. Hence the rose breeder, as well as looking for new colors and habits, is constantly seeking the disease-free rose, while the aster breeder's quest is to create cultivars impervious to aster wilt disease.

Hybrid plants resulting from the crossing of two parents, either accidentally or deliberately, are known as the F_1 generation. Many F_1 hybrids of known parents, especially among annuals and bedding plants, are much sought after for their uniformity, strength of constitution, and long flowering period. These F_1 hybrids can be produced under controlled conditions; this involves isolating them from other species with which they could hybridize accidentally, excluding from them all visiting pollinating insects, and often removing the male or female sexual parts. F_1 hybrids do not come true from seed. Each time a new batch of F_1 hybrid seed is required, this labor-intensive process of production has to be undertaken afresh, which is why F_1 hybrid seed is always more expensive.

The following generation is called the F_2 generation. These plants can sometimes be attractive enough in their own right to be worth growing, or they may be quite inferior, depending on how the breeding has worked out.

scrutiny, and are at the mercy of cold, heat, drought, flooding, and other natural conditions likely to be faced in a garden situation. It would be pointless to pamper a prospective newcomer on the trial ground, only for it to fail miserably when grown by the average gardener. Given this tough treatment, it gradually becomes apparent which plants are the likely winners.

Before new varieties can be made available to the public, all new stock must be built up in sufficient quantity to satisfy initial demand, although for the first year or two after the launch of particularly noteworthy introductions, demand often exceeds supply. To make the new flowers available to all, the seed must be harvested in adequate quantities; herbaceous perennials must be propagated by division or cuttings in their thousands; most roses, and many trees and shrubs, must be budded or grafted on to special rootstocks for strong growth and rapid re-establishment.

In the future the supply of new flowers to an expectant market will be significantly improved by use of micropropagation. In this technique, very small pieces of plant tissue are removed from the parent and grown on in a special nutrient medium to produce a large mass of cellular propagation material. This is then converted into tiny plantlets by dividing it up into many sections and growing it on (raising it in) a different nutrient gel. This process is revolutionizing plant production on a massive scale. Micropropagated plants are already available in garden centers and are improving year by year. Each season sees new varieties of rose offered for sale on their own roots, the result of this high-tech form of propagation, but they are not the only plants now to be produced in this way as more and more "test-tube babies" join them.

Many new plants are subject to "Plant Patents," a type of copyright in respect of the raiser or the company introducing a new plant to the market, who is paid a certain sum each time a plant is propagated. To produce plants from such stock without regard to this payment is to breach this recognition of the breeder.

The way in which new cultivars are named varies. Many are named after the raiser, his or her relations,

THE RED DELPHINIUM, WHICH HAS BEEN ACHIEVED AFTER MANY years of effort by the breeders.

the home town, and so on, and some breeders are willing to name their "babies" after notable people, or a consumer product. Sometimes charitable organizations have plants named for them, and will usually receive a certain sum per plant in the same way as a breeder or company gets a Plant Patent. Often the raiser or breeder makes a charge for the privilege of naming a plant after a person – this can be several thousand dollars.

The success of a new plant depends to a large extent on how it is promoted, but to become a classic favorite for decades to come, the variety must continue to perform well and stay in fashion. When the Hybrid Tea rose 'Peace' was introduced after the second world war, it became an immediate favorite, at first because of the fairy-tale story of its introduction – first budded in France in 1936, it was smuggled out to the United States during the war – and its full, yellow, pink-edged bloom. Nearly half a century later, its popularity has hardly diminished. Not only have the flowers maintained their fashion-ability, but the variety remains one of the strongest in cultivation.

'Super Star' was all set to do the same. A strong-growing, healthy rose with a totally new color – a luminous vermilion – it took the rose-buying public by storm. Now, three decades later, it is a disease-prone shadow of its former self, and the violent shades of its blooms are unacceptable for the gentler color schemes of today.

Although this book is called *New Flowers*, it looks not only at new cultivars but also at new trends in planting. Bedding geraniums, begonias, busy lizzies, pansies, and the like have become so easy to raise from seed that they have become part of the "throwaway society." Instead of overwintering these perennials as stock plants or rooted cuttings, they are frequently discarded after flowering, to be raised anew the following spring.

While the search goes on for still more new forms of our favorite garden plants, our awareness of environmental issues has produced a widespread interest in the planting of natural species, not only in wild areas, but alongside more conventional garden flowers. "Old-fashioned" species roses, and modern, shrubby forms developed from these, are vying for pride of place in the border with the more formal Large-flowered roses (Hybrid Teas) and Cluster-flowered types (Floribundas).

Gardening is a burgeoning industry, yet gardens are getting smaller, and becoming extensions to the home. The garden is now a place in which to relax and socialize, rather than just a place in which to grow flowers. This has necessitated the search for plants that are attractive over as long a period as possible; perennials requiring minimum staking; compact shrubs; roses and trees that never outgrow their situation.

The demands of modern living mean that while more people own gardens, they have less time to look after them. This has resulted in the development of low-maintenance gardens – ornamental paving and gravel often taking the place of the lawn and flowers being newly used to provide ground cover in mass plantings. Impatience of spirit also means that for

many people it is not acceptable to wait ten years or more for a desired plant to flower, thus the breeding of early-maturing forms is demanded by the gardening public. Container growing has made it possible for planting to take place nearly all year round, and for consumers to buy and plant the subject in full flower.

It is impossible in a book of this kind to cover comprehensively everything new in the world of flowers. But it does attempt to inspire gardeners by including as many of the best examples of plant development and gardening trends as possible.

For the future, the most likely and far-reaching developments would seem to lie in the field of genetic engineering, in which the plant genes are manipulated to alter substantially the characteristics of the subject. It is an emotive topic, and while most experimentation of this nature is at present merely an extension of the plant breeder's work in producing the most vigorous and attractive newcomers, in time it is likely that we shall see, as common constituents of our own flower borders, genetic crosses between unrelated genera. Perhaps future editions of this book will contain the progeny of crosses between roses and rhododendrons.

Viola 'Jolly Joker', a pansy in an unusual color combination, is a vibrant newcomer.

ANNUALS AND BEDDING PLANTS

Summer bedding designs rely heavily on annuals to bring showy variety to the garden. Of these familiar, often gaudy blooms, surprisingly few are native to the cool shores of Europe or the temperate zones of North America, but instead hail from more exotic climes.

Due to the energy and enthusiasm of nurserymen and scientists, gardeners everywhere now have a wide choice of color, variety, and size in the popular annuals. The hybrids have also had their characteristic traits developed and diversified, so that they are now more tolerant of cooler weather and more resistant to disease than the native species.

Even the conventional hard work and careful cultivation that the old annuals required has been reduced. Greenhouse techniques, daunting to the gardener with little time and unavailable to most city dwellers, are no longer an essential part of the routine cultivation of annuals. Thanks to the advanced technology of plant breeding, it is now possible to obtain young seedlings and plantlets direct from the seed companies.

The range of bedding plants available has been significantly increased by the growing practice of using plants such as gazanias, which are technically perennials, as annuals. Additionally, perennials such as pelargoniums, which were once used for bedding, and lifted and kept indoors over the winter, are now much easier to raise from seed.

AN ANNUAL BORDER DISPLAYING STRONG SWATHES OF BRIGHT new color from a mixture of hybrid tagetes and dianthus.

MARIGOLDS

The bitter odor associated with French and African marigolds – properly known as *Tagetes* – has been removed from some of the newer hybrids, and in others the distinctive bright gold tones have been bleached to a snowy white. The blooms of these garden stalwarts are now produced in a wide range of sizes, from the neat, compact head of the semi-dwarf varieties to tightly ruffled blooms up to 4 inches (10 cm) wide, in flamboyant doubles and simple singles.

There are hybrids in which the unusual tail, a characteristic of the *Tagetes* seed, has been bred away, and this makes for easier planting. And there are "mule" marigolds which, not enfeebled by seed production, bloom and bloom and bloom.

All this botanical engineering has been inspired by the great popularity of *Tagetes*, which is described as "radiant, versatile, and easy to grow." They can be planted to glow in a garden bed, or to create a stunning color patch in patio containers. Folk wisdom recommends that they be placed as a border plant for roses to fight off black spot.

Closely related to *Tagetes*, and sharing many of its attributes, is the pot marigold *Calendula*. It, too, has been extensively bred to provide a wide range of doubles, semidoubles, and dwarfs in a range of yellows, oranges, golds, and even reds.

THE FULLY DOUBLE BLOOM OF 'Sugar and Spice' (left) is the first ever white marigold. Scientists have long desired to achieve this remarkable bleaching of the traditional and determined brilliance of the Tagetes.

The large, single flowers of 'Disco Orange' (above) are strongly recommended for bedding and patio displays, where their ability to withstand inclement weather and their long blooming period give a pleasant dash of color all summer.

'TOUCH OF RED', A VARIETY OF the pot marigold Calendula, makes a showy and uncommon display of apricot, primrose, pale gold, and flame red (right). It is a productive plant, and the large, graceful blooms bear well-frilled petals. This marigold grows to a height of 12 inches (30 cm) and when planted en masse makes a firm, solid border to taller bedding plants, or can be planted in an informal, wild-looking arrangement such as the one illustrated.

SWEET PEAS AND BEGONIAS

The sweet pea, *Lathyrus*, is, and has been since Victorian times, a great favorite in the flower garden. The climbing or trailing stems carry many scented blooms that are delightful as cut flowers. But breeding has altered the old tall plants grown against stakes and trellises, and the modern gardener can purchase dwarf varieties that grow to a mere 12 inches (30 cm), which makes them perfect for edging a border and for the small city garden.

Breeders continue to make subtle changes in the colors of sweet peas, hoping to find really strong hues such as deep purple and royal blue in place of the more common pastels, and have changed the blooms from single to furled and doubled, curled and crimped, often with colored edgings or mottlings on the petals. Some of these alterations may be too subtle for the ordinary eye to detect, but the great lovers and breeders of sweet peas note these changes with enthusiasm. Much attention has also been paid to improving the fragrance of the flowers.

Sweet peas thrive in a deeply dug and well-composted soil that is ideally slightly alkaline. They grow best in cool weather. To assist germination, many gardeners recommend that each seed be "chipped" with a sharp knife before planting.

The modern varieties of fibrous-rooted *Begonia* are bred as "easy-to-grow" subjects for the annual border and the hanging basket. As with sweet peas, the range of single shades and bicolors increases year by year, and there are now new subtle hues to add to the traditional primary yellows and reds. The leaves are as attractive as the flowers, and in the new varieties may be bronze or purple, with a rich, strong gloss; they look excellent at all times, even when the plant is not in bloom.

GARDEN STYLE GUIDE

Make use of the natural climbing abilities of sweet peas by growing them up a trellis or arbor. The new dwarf varieties can be planted in hanging baskets or used as a ground cover in spring and early summer.

Begonias make a fine show in annual bedding designs. Except in cool areas they prefer a site out of the full sun.

AN ENTIRELY NEW EFFECT HAS been created for the urban garden in the short Lathyrus odoratus *'Dwarf Patio Mixed' (left). It could be used as an edging plant or be container-grown to excellent effect.*

RICH, DARK AND GLOSSY FOLIAGE with a bronze tone has been combined with the abundant pale blooms of Begonia semperflorens *'White Devil' (right). This partnership makes for an effect of strong, eye-catching contrasts in a mass bedding design.*

PINKS

Dianthus chinensis, the China, Indian, or "annual" pink is an asset in any garden. Grown en masse the clusters of pink and crimson blooms make a delightful sea of color over an extended flowering period. A true perennial, but now usually treated as an annual, the *chinensis* can offer a long, untroubled, and disease-free life.

These pinks are the ones most commonly grown outdoors, especially in North America. Native to many parts of the world, they have a long history in cultivation, although at one time they were not easy to grow in any but the most temperate climates. However, modern hybridization has overcome the difficulties, and the plants now adorn many gardens throughout Europe and North America.

Dianthus chinensis hybrids have been bred to retain the flower's traditional charm, evocative perfume, and subtle foliage. The new hybrids have strong colors and a stocky, almost bushy shape. The loose clusters of low-lying blooms persuade most gardeners to use it as a pretty edging plant or as spots of delightful color focus in rock gardens. Their lack of height allows these flowers to edge almost any bed of annuals, but the pinks and wine reds of the newest varieties are possibly best enjoyed when separated into their own tubs or pots.

China pinks prefer a well-drained soil that is not acid, and they thrive where lime is present, although this is not an essential ingredient. Frequent deadheading helps to extend the flowering period, but some of the newer hybrids do not even need this simple treatment.

The flowering period usually extends from July to October. The new hybrids do prefer sunny spots and are strongly recommended for window boxes as a cheerful display for any apartment dweller.

--- **GARDEN STYLE GUIDE** ---

The dianthus is admired not only for its bright flowers but also for its attractive foliage. The new varieties add greatly to a "cottage garden" effect, or can be used to soften the hard edges of a patio. Plant dianthus where their perfume can be fully appreciated. Fill a wide ceramic pot with them and place it near an often-used entrance.

THE FRINGED PETALS OF THE Dianthus chinensis *are emphasized in this F₁ picotee hybrid (left) of strong contrasts. These plants will tolerate heat and rain, thus guaranteeing continual outdoor color. The lance-shaped leaves in a subtle green are an added attraction, and this makes a superb cut flower.*

LOOSELY CLUSTERED, FRILLED, and open, with deep blush centers that fade to paler hue, these F₁ hybrid 'Blush Crimson' pinks create a rich, yet delicate carpet of color (right) more subtle than the intense monotone of the 'Single Rose' blooms (left). Grown outdoors, treat Dianthus chinensis *as half-hardy and set young plants out after last frost. These charming plants can also be grown indoors in pots and can be persuaded to bloom for most of the year.*

ZINNIAS

Zinnia is a perfect example of an annual that brings clear color to temperate gardens, yet it is a native of a warm and exotic clime. Its bold, almost vulgar appearance is not always appreciated, but for many the zinnia is a joyous, plebeian flower firmly proclaiming its origins in hot, dusty Mexico.

The hybrid zinnia has been bred to enhance the lovely variety of its natural color. Botanists have developed the flower into impressive double blooms, such as the 'Tetra Ruffled Jumbo', in which the flower face measures 6 inches (15 cm) across. Dwarf specimens have also been bred, and these bring a note of sharp gaiety to a small city garden. Other new forms include cactus-flowered types, while the latest color range embraces an unusual shade of chartreuse green.

Treat zinnias as half-hardy annuals. Rather than buying seedlings or ready-grown plants, which are usually restricted in their range, it is better to grow the new varieties from seed. In temperate climates, seeds should be sown in late March in the warmth, but in the warmer zones of North America they can be sown directly outdoors. Remember that most zinnias dislike humidity.

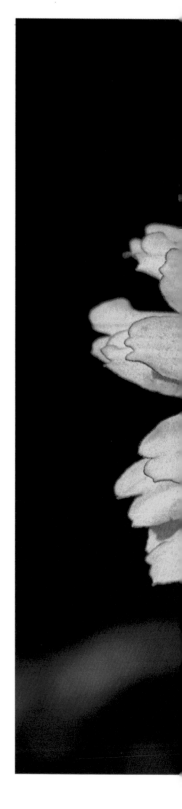

DWARF ZINNIAS, SUCH AS THE 'Miniature Pom-Pom' (left), give a wonderful display as bedding plants or on a patio.

THE COLOR COMBINATIONS bred into the latest full-size hybrids are so spectacular – gaudy even – that 'Whirligig' (right) and similar blooms deserve their own bed to display them to advantage. Cut zinnias often, not only because they are superb in arrangements, but also because this will increase their blooming capacity. The tall varieties, especially, look magnificent in vases.

PETUNIAS

Modern petunias are a far cry from the native Argentinian species. With gardeners in mind, botanists have produced a bewildering number of choices in both color and size. The funnel-shaped flowers come with smooth, monochrome petals or huge, showy, ruffled blooms and in various heights.

Petunias can be relied upon to bloom all summer, but they do tend to look bedraggled and limp in wet weather. This trait, however, is under seige, and some of the latest hybrids, such as the Double Multifloras, are described as "rain-resistant", and retain a firm appearance even when they are damp.

The amazing selection of hybrid colors and shapes can create a small garden brimming with a variety of petunia textures and hues. However, such a garden could be a lifetime's work, for there are literally hundreds of hybrids to select from. Less experienced gardeners are best advised to start with those plants that are bred for their size and vigor.

Because petunias come in such an extensive range of colors they can be considered for almost any garden color scheme.

GARDEN STYLE GUIDE

There are petunias that stand 24 inches (60 cm) tall and others that remain under 12 inches (30 cm). This gives them fine versatility in the garden. Excellent as bedding plants, they make a gorgeous display filling a windowbox or tumbling from a hanging basket. The petunia is at its largest and most flamboyant in the gigantically double-frilled Grandifloras, but all types should be deadheaded regularly.

THE UNUSUAL COLOR arrangements of the hybrid petunia are typified by the broadly marked Petunia grandiflora *'Red Star' (above), and the soft white heart of the 'Rose Dawn' (left). The breeders' effects on petal shape are also demonstrated in these examples, one having a frilled edge, the other, the 'Red Star', bearing a clean line to its petals.*

VARIETIES OF THE LARGE-bloomed Petunia grandiflora *are ideal for tubs and hanging baskets. This delicately veined 'Peppermint' makes an emphatic color point on the patio or gives a cheerful edging to a bed of summer annuals.*

THE GRANDIFLORA HYBRID 'Blush Pink' (below) suits a garden plan of gentle tones and pastel hues. The thick cluster appearance of the blooms is suited to borders, but can also look wonderful bursting out of and over a ceramic tub.

PETUNIAS

Petunias will thrive in almost any conditions, once they have passed the delicate seedling stage. The seed is very small and needs to be planted with some care in fine, level soil. The future hardiness of the plants is helped if they are transplanted twice indoors before being moved outdoors.

The latest hybrids are described in the catalogues as "easy to grow," but many of these have been hand pollinated by the nurserymen and this makes them expensive to purchase. However, this initial investment will be well rewarded by their display.

The hybrids bloom throughout the summer, and the satiny flowers, produced in great profusion, are a constant pleasure. The soft texture of the petals brings a subtle hue to the rich reds, pinks, and purples common to the petunia.

Although petunias are most often associated with purples and reds, their range has been extended to indigo blues, ice-cream pinks, snowy whites, and even pale yellows. In its simple, single form, or as one of the new double varieties, it is a flower that can be included in most color arrangements. The differing growth and shape of the various hybrids also adds to its versatility in the garden design. Some grow in mounds of blossom, others tend to trail a little – these are ideal for the hanging basket – yet others stand fairly erect.

Although petunia breeders have largely concentrated their attentions on the flowers, there are some varieties in which the foliage is improved from its unspectacular norm, with larger, sometimes marked and delicately veined leaves.

THE DOUBLE MULTIFLORA IS A petunia of showy blossoms. The three examples of 'Giant Victorious Mixed' shown here reveal som of the many petal variations that have been bred into these popular hybrids.

BOTANISTS HAVE BECOME ARTISTS with their breeding programs, and have created strange and lovely color forms, such as this gently shaded petunia (right), a subtle advance on the bold tones of earlier hybrids.

ANTIRRHINUMS

The traditional velvet snout and curling jaw of the flowering "dragon" have long been favorites in cultivation, but botanists have now bred *Antirrhinum* hybrids with wide, open florets that scarcely warrant the name of "snapdragon". These new forms are often open throated, and if the mysterious closed look has been lost, then the exposure of color in the deep inner tubes gives these butterfly-flowered hybrids their new interest.

Apart from opening and flattening the florets, science has also given the antirrhinum an extended flowering season. Many varieties have also been bred as fine cutting flowers, which can be relied upon to last well in floral arrangements. Colors, too, have been extended and formalized: not only is there a rich variety of shades, but these are blended so that the gardener can be sure of growing the hue preferred in any garden design.

Although the antirrhinum is botanically a perennial, it has now been developed for use as an annual. Rust disease once ravaged antirrhinum populations, but new strains have been developed to provide solid resistance to this blight. Even so, it is wise to avoid planting antirrhinums in beds previously occupied by *Alcea (Althaea)*, *Lavatera*, or *Dianthus*, which can act as hosts to the rust disease.

'LITTLE DARLING' IS A SUPERB example of the dwarf hybrid. The floret is open throated and the shape is referred to as "butterfly", for the fluttering open petals have lost their "snap". It comes in a rich variety of colors.

This hybrid has many sturdy qualities – an early-starting, long flowering period, resistance to rust disease, and ease in cultivation. These traits have won awards for the hybrid on both sides of the Atlantic.

As with all antirrhinums, frequent deadheading does help prolong the flowering period considerably.

GARDEN STYLE GUIDE

Antirrhinums naturally love rocks and brick walls, but their cheerful color keeps them popular as bedding plants. The taller plants give drama to the garden and their bright hues are best displayed against gray foliage. Blended with the golden tones of heleniums, backed by the blues of delphiniums, the new dwarf antirrhinum excels as a border plant.

All antirrhinums will do best if placed in full sun and in rich, well-drained soil, but they will also thrive in windowboxes and other containers to provide a long season of color.

THE PLANTS OF THE DWARF hybrid 'Floral Carpet', shown in two variations (left), are so vigorous that they are like a ground cover imbued with rich mounds of color.

'MAGIC CARPET MIXED' (BELOW) has the traditional look of the "dragon" combined with vigorous growth.

LOBELIAS AND NEMESIAS

Scattered through the tall and colorful specimens that inhabit a bed of annuals, low, delicate clumps of small blooms will form a vital base and provide visual emphasis. Both *Lobelia* and *Nemesia* serve this purpose as edging and bedding plants.

The new varieties of nemesia bring a wide range of gently subtle colors, whereas the lobelia offers a strong contrast of blues, crimsons, or sharp white. The latter plant is a great favorite for borders, although it does not like hot weather and needs a humus-enriched soil if it is to thrive. Many of the new lobelia hybrids seek to vary the length of the stems and to extend the color range.

Breeders have worked to alter the shape of both these clump-forming plants by creating semi-creeping or trailing plants with wider garden uses. The lobelia, in particular, can now be planted to trail from a hanging basket or tumble over a ceramic container placed on the patio.

Nemesias are reasonably easy to grow but do not like high heat or humidity. To induce bushiness in this plant, it is worth pinching out the seedlings. Grown in this manner, the multicolored blooms make a splendid display in the mild summer garden.

THE LOBELIA TENUIOR *WAS ONCE preferred as a pot plant, but the hybrid 'Blue Wings' (above) withstands outdoor living and blooms all summer. The deep indigo blue of the petals verges on purple.*

A GORGEOUS ARRAY OF BRIGHT colors presented in staggered heights is held within an edging of lobelias. Despite the powerful blue and white tones used in this border, the effect is softened through the delicacy of lobelia's blooms on their well-bred, slender stems.

THE LOOSE DELICACY OF NEMESIA is enhanced by intermingling shades and colors of the hybrid 'Tapestry', making it a superb addition to the plant's range (right).

CELOSIAS

Gardeners who prefer muted shades may be loath to introduce the brilliance of annuals to their garden. Yet, placed against gray or neutral foliage, a patch of intense color will provide a visual relief in the most subtle garden design. The powerful hues of *Celosia* hybrids will certainly create suitable drama.

Their fiery tones of gold, yellow, and crimson immediately draw the eye, but this does not mean that these wonderful flowers have to be separated from the other annuals in the summer garden. Celosias can be grown in bold designs or with the multicolored blooms of the salpiglossis, which help to absorb some of their tonal impact.

The heads of these flowers can be crested as in *Celosia cristata*, or plumed as in *Celosia plumosa*, and plants come in heights varying from 9 to 24 inches (23 to 30 cm). The unusual shapes of the blooms bring a note of luxury to the flowerbed. A half-hardy annual, celosia flowers between July and September. The seedlings should be raised indoors and planted out when danger of frost has gone and nights are 60°F. (15°C.) or higher.

Ideally, celosias prefer warm, southerly climates, but the hybridization of these plants has led to greater growing success and a certain hardiness even in temperate zones. Celosias are currently being bred into more vigorous plants with a considerably longer blooming period, and in an expanding range of colors, including some more muted shades that are easier to work with.

Celosias thrive in sunny beds, but will also survive in partial shade.

THE DARING GARDENER CAN juxtapose the glorious golds of the newest celosias with the regal purple of salvia (above) in an avant-garde bedding design. Alternatively they can be massed in a bed.

SOME CELOSIA HYBRIDS HAVE been endowed with heavy plumes and a wide variety of hues – deep gold, pure scarlet, and a subtle orange – as in these perfect specimens of 'Century Mixed' (right).

GARDEN STYLE GUIDE

A mass planting of celosias will create a vivid area of color. Since it has been bred in varying heights, the celosia can now be used either as a border plant or intermingled with other plants in the general show of a summer bed. The silky, feathery plumes of celosia make fine dried displays.

*THE COCKSCOMB (*CELOSIA cristata) *is a weird bloom which, in the hybrid form of 'Olympia Mixed', offers a feast of rich color tones (left and overleaf). Another good cultivar is 'Jewel Box Mixed.'*

LAVATERAS

Lavatera trimestra is a naturally tall plant which, in its natural form can grow as high as 48 inches (1.2 m), but this is not a height that suits the average urban garden.

Hybridization has created a new lavatera that is only 24 inches (60 cm) tall, and this delightful bushy plant is now easily accommodated in the annual bedding scheme. Other qualities, such as the ability to survive most weather conditions and to withstand wind, have also been developed.

The glory of the lavatera is the trumpet-shaped bloom which, in the newest hybrids, has assumed a glistening effect in the petal color. The flowers are held singly in the axis of the upper leaves, and the whole plant forms a glossy green mound richly decorated with blooms.

Lavatera is generally best sown indoors in April, then thinned and planted out in May. The seedlings or the seeds – for they can also be grown in situ in warm areas – should be placed about 24 inches (60 cm) apart, since these little bushes need ample space in which to spread.

——— **GARDEN STYLE GUIDE** ———

The bushy habit of the lavatera makes it an ideal specimen for the back of low-growing borders, where it forms a rich background texture and shields its neighbors from the wind. The clear pale pinks look good with campanulas, hollyhocks, and scabious. Clumps of the hybrid 'Mont Blanc' will create an intense white interlude among brighter colors or, grown as a cluster, will create a solid eye-catching effect.

'SILVER CUP' (BELOW) IS ONE OF the newest lavatera hybrids and bears a great profusion of flowers. In order to enjoy its appealing bicolored blooms for as long as possible, the gardener should be sure to keep the plants moist and frequently deadhead the spent and faded blooms.

THE PART-TIME GARDENER WILL appreciate the shimmering white of 'Mont Blanc' (right) in a garden that is usually seen at the end of the day in the dusk. It is best not to use too rich a soil for the lavatera since this tends to thicken the foliage and detract from the glamour of the bloom.

POPPIES

Poppies are a delightful adornment in any garden, and are romantic plants, evoking lovely rural summers tinged by the sad shadow of young men fallen in war.

Far removed from the traditional scarlet, many of the new *Papaver* hybrids produce large blossoms of pastel pinks, yellows, and golds, and also soft reds. The flower, with its wide, tissue-paper petals, is borne upright on a stem that can reach 48 inches (1.2 m) in height, yet, because of the delicacy of the bloom, these do not need staking. Rather, they should be allowed to adopt their own delightful natural stance.

Dead blooms should be removed frequently to prolong the flowering season. Once this is over, the unsightly foliage on the spent poppies should be cut down before it becomes an eyesore.

Two species of *Papaver* have been widely bred for summer in the garden. *Papaver nudicaule*, the Iceland poppy, is, at heart, a short-lived perennial, but is now treated as a hardy annual or biennial, whereas *Papaver rhoeas* is naturally an annual. Both thrive in sun or light shade, and any reasonable garden soil will sustain them. Poppies dislike being transplanted, so the seeds should be sown directly in position in early spring. The mature plants will bloom from late May to July.

The Iceland poppy is, of all the *Papaver* species, the one most suited to cut-flower arrangements. Cut flowers of the new varieties while still in bud and sear each stem with a flame or plunge it into boiling water to prolong the life of the blooms. A milky white substance flows out of the stem – the source of opium in some species.

THE BEAUTY OF THE PETALS AND colors bred into 'Windsong' look most effective when gathered in groups or clusters. Other unusual new varieties available, such as 'Mother of Pearl', come in a range of more subtle shades, including pale pinks, mauves, grays, and apricots.

THE YELLOW PAPAVER *nudicaule 'Windsong' (left) exaggerates the crumpled tissue-paper look, so characteristic of the poppy. This 'Windsong' hybrid has been bred to emphasize the silky sheen of the wide, colorful petals that are a natural attribute of the Icelandic poppy. The seed heads can be cut and dried for winter arrangement.*

GARDEN STYLE GUIDE

The *Papaver* looks best when grown in clumps, where the wide, silky petals in new, delicate shades will flutter in a loosely gathered mass of color. Also, this makes them easier to cut down when the foliage turns ugly later in the season. The bed can then be used for spring plants. Place poppies so that their pleasing display can be viewed from the house, but be careful where you place them if children are likely to play in the garden, since all parts of the plant are poisonous.

The new dwarf varieties, such as 'Garden Gnome Mixed,' would make unusual edging plants for a border.

NICOTIANAS

The *Nicotiana*, or tobacco plant, despite the prettiness of its flowers, has not always been a great favorite in the garden, for the older varieties had the annoying habit of closing their petals during the day and opening them at night. They also grew long, awkward stems. Careful experimentation has produced dwarf varieties on which the scented, star-shaped flowers stay open and fragrant all day. Now, in hybrid form the nicotiana grows as a neat, bushy plant, smothered in blooms. The hybrids retain the wonderful fragrance of the native plant, which is particularly intense at night.

The new hybrids prefer to be grown in moist soil in a partially shaded area, but will also thrive in the sun as long as it is not too intense. Nicotianas can be sown using the half-hardy annual technique, or they can be sown directly out-of-doors in situ in mid-April. The spent flowers should be deadheaded frequently to maintain a successive profusion of blooms all summer long.

Plant nicotianas where their exquisite scent can be fully appreciated – along a path or near the garden sitting area. They are wonderful plants in the informal flowerbed and equally pleasing grown in large clumps, near white bedding verbenas, or with trailing blue lobelias.

The colorful trumpet blooms are also decorative in ceramic tubs on the patio or window ledge and, indoors, bring a graceful element to cut-flower arrangements.

A BED OF NICOTIANA *'NICKI Mixed' (left) shows the variety of color available in these scented, free-flowering hybrids. 'Nicki Mixed' grow to 16 inches (40 cm) and produce seven different colors. The fresh 'Lime Green' (above left) brings a pleasing green flower to the garden, and its hue is bright enough to lift the bloom from its surrounding foliage.*

THE PURITY OF NICOTIANA *'Domino White' emphasizes the pretty star-shaped bloom. Because the nicotiana hybrids are long flowering, these white blossoms can act as a foil to the bright colors of both spring and summer beds.*

CLARKIA, LOVE-IN-A-MIST, AND SCABIOUS

The three annuals *Clarkia*, *Scabiosa*, and *Nigella* share the attributes of graceful, pretty blossoms and ease of growing. All three can be grown from seed sown directly on site in April, with plants thinned out as necessary during May.

The newest hybrids of *Clarkia elegans* present plants that are vigorous and sturdy in growth, and this makes them accessible to even the most inexperienced gardener. The most pleasing developments include the hybrids' capacity to produce full and heavy blooms along the entire length of their stems, and an increased compactness of form. Sow them near godetias or *Centaurea cyanus*.

The native *Scabiosa* was not always a favorite in the garden, for its bloom of deep crimson had a sad and limp appearance. However, hybridization has concentrated on producing a wonderful variety of colors on blossoms that are joyously frilled and furled. New dwarf varieties, and those with bronze seed heads, excellent for drying, are other welcome additions to the range.

Love-in-a-mist, or nigella, naturally a cornflower blue, has also been bred to produce blossoms of many delicate colors in the hues of old porcelain. The graceful, fernlike foliage makes it an excellent filler in the border.

THE SLENDER FOLIAGE FORMS A lacy background to the soft petals and coroneted seed globes of nigella. The bushy growth of this N. hispanica *'Atlantica' brings form and grace to the border and an airy elegance to the garden.*

THE DEEPLY LOBED LEAVES OF scabious make it excellent for massing in the garden and for cutting. The plant can grow to 36 inches (90 cm) and needs discreet support. This hybrid named 'Stella' shows the flamboyant beauty of the new, fully double flowers.

'ROYAL BOUQUET' (RIGHT) IS A hybrid that fully exploits the grace and beauty of Clarkia elegans. *The species can be grown in a wild flower garden, but the racemes of the hybrid give a much grander show and well deserve a more formal setting.*

GAZANIAS

The sprawling, tumbling *Gazania* is a perfect border annual. Its bright, sunny flowers reflect the warm climate of its native South Africa, where it is no longer known in its pure form even in the wild for it has interbred with other species. And now gazanias have also been scientifically hybridized for garden use across the world.

Although botanically a perennial, the gazania should be treated as a half-hardy annual and planted in well-drained soil. It flowers from June to September and makes a charming show in borders and rock gardens. Here the new vigorous varieties will grow to about 6 inches (15 cm) high.

The flower has a daisy-like quality and closes as the sun sets. It is borne on a plant perfectly designed as a low rambler, for as each bloom lifts its face upward to the sun, the petals reveal an interesting pattern of color which the breeders have enhanced in a variety of colors from black to green. The leaves are narrow and bred to be variegated in some new varieties; the foliage is thick enough to form a backdrop on which blooms are studded like stars.

THE NEWEST GAZANIAS OFFER A good range of color, from the warm pink of 'Magenta Green' (above) to the candy stripes of 'Suttons Hybrids' (left and right). The narrow leaves, with their silky silver undersides, add to the attraction of these bright blooms. The petal markings of these picturesque miniature garden flowers give them a "designer" quality that scientists have worked to emphasize and vary.

The characteristics of gazanias are enhanced when plants are placed in a rock garden and the stems forced to fall over a wall of gray granite or red brick.

The busy lizzie, or *Impatiens*, is a long-time favorite summer bedding plant that has now been bred in an increasing array of colors and forms. Busy lizzies are half-hardy perennials grown as annuals in all but frost-free climates, mostly from F_1 hybrid seed. The increasing popularity and success of these plants as small, colorful garden flowers is testimony to the scientists' skill in creating new plants with more hardy features.

In moist, semishaded areas, busy lizzies will provide a low sheet of color over a long period. Unlike their predecessors, the new F_1 hybrids will all stand full sun, even in hot areas. For a flowering season that lasts from late spring until October, start seeds indoors six to eight weeks before the last frost.

The newest ranges of hybrids come in a wide selection of colors, including an unusual blue shade, and many have the "eye" of the bloom picked out in a contrasting color. There are also striped varieties. The flowers may be single or double and there are some dwarf hybrids.

GARDEN STYLE GUIDE

The breeders have considered practicalities in developing their new hybrid versions of impatiens, which give reliable and consistent performance all summer.

These are a delight in tubs, hanging baskets, or growing in the border close to the muted tones of compact gray-leaved plants such as varieties of senecio or euphorbia.

BREEDERS HAVE ENSURED THAT despite the small stature of the impatiens the blooms are large and sharp with color. The low-growing habits of the busy lizzie can be exploited to give a wide swathe of color in the garden (left).

OUTSTANDING AMONG THE F_1 hybrids of impatiens is the Accent Bright Eye series. These flowers have been bred to attain a diameter of more than 2 inches (5 cm). They come in a spectrum of colors that includes pure white (right) and a clear, stunning red (above), along with many other shades in the pink to purple range.

PELARGONIUMS

The *Pelargonium* is a tender South African herb that is now a much-loved garden flower all over the world. Since being transplanted from its native land, it has undergone many changes and has come to be commonly – and incorrectly – known as the "geranium." Pelargoniums are of three types, the Zonals, typified by zoned markings on the leaves; Regals, with larger flowers and now bred to flower repeatedly all season; and the Ivy-leaved, which are semiprostrate types.

The pelargonium provides natural assistance to the breeder by the fact that there is much natural "sporting" or mutation. This has the most marked effect on the leaf variegation, but can also create new color patterns on the petals. The latest hybrids are bred to be grown from seed and thrive as half-hardy annuals in temperate areas. The breeders have also experimented with its form, producing plants as small as 5 inches (12.5 cm) or as tall as 72 inches (1.8 m). Pelargoniums are upright or tumbling, and the natural bright crimsons and vermilions have been extended into pastel hues and variegated combinations. The blossoms are single or double. Leaves have been bred in a multitude of variegated forms, and with a variety of subtle scents.

--------- **GARDEN STYLE GUIDE** ---------

The pelargonium is at its best when planted to create a focal point. Group numbers of them together in formal bedding designs, or crowd them into their own urn or windowbox. This plant has become an essential part of the hanging basket arrangement, but care should be taken with color planning, since some of the tones of this flower can be very sharp.

MULTIBLOOMS, A NEW GROUP OF Zonal pelargonium hybrids have been bred to be grown from seed and to flower very early. Colors include delicate new shades such as 'Lavender' (above) and the intense strident tones of the hybrid 'Scarlet Eye' (left).

THE SPECTACULAR CHANGES THAT modern techniques have brought to the pelargonium are displayed in the Zonal hybrid 'Apple Blossom' (right). Here the naturally flat, open face of the native bloom has become a tightly clustered rosebud shape.

COSMOS, HIBISCUS, AND ANAGALLIS

Cosmos, Hibiscus, and *Anagallis* are three vigorous bedding plants whose new varieties are worthy of a place in the summer garden. The petals of the latest strains of cosmos, which may be shaded or striped in a contrasting color, are delicate in hue, even when they feature rich pinks or golds. In contrast, the latest hibiscus varieties, with their sturdy, bushlike qualities and mat leaves have been bred to emphasize the colored center of the bloom.

Anagallis, the pimpernel, shares features with both cosmos and hibiscus, for though its blooms are dainty, the plant carries an intrepid strength in its form and shape. This herb has traditionally been used for medicinal purposes, but the hybridizers have concentrated on developing a pleasing bedding plant in a good range of colors for the summer garden.

If the cosmos is started indoors in April and planted out after the risk of frost is past, it will bloom in July and should continue to bloom profusely until the first frost of fall.

The varieties of bedding hibiscus have largely been bred from tender species that once would grow only in the protected environment of the greenhouse or conservatory. Although hardy enough to grow outdoors, these plants demand care in their early stages to ensure that they are properly hardened off. The many new varieties of *Hibiscus moscheutos* grow well in temperate climates.

GARDEN STYLE GUIDE

The variety of color in the cosmos range adds a bright note whether plants are used on their own or interplanted with others. It is an excellent flower for cutting.

Any patio garden will be enhanced by an hibiscus bush in a tub, but neater new varieties of plants can be grouped to form a small cluster in the garden.

ANAGALLIS ARVENSIS *(ABOVE) IS a good rock garden and bedding plant. The flowers of this hybrid, a marked contrast to the scarlet of its parents, feature small, fringed petals.*

THE *fluted petals of the cosmos hybrid 'Sea Shells' (left) are crimson with pink interiors, but this hybrid also comes in monotone pinks.*

THE HIBISCUS MOSCHEUTOS F_1 *hybrid 'Disco Belle White' (right) displays the highly bred perfection of the trumpet bloom.*

SALPIGLOSSIS, GAILLARDIA, AND MIMULUS

Salpiglossis, Gaillardia, and *Mimulus* are three annuals that offer some of the richest colors in the summer garden, and yet these have been further enhanced by the efforts of the breeders.

In salpiglossis, attention has been concentrated on the lovely bloom. The result is that in the latest varieties the flowers have become intricately stitched and overlaid with satiny, subtle color. The foliage remains thin and unobtrusive, the better to display the bloom. Dwarf hybrids, growing to no more than 12 inches (30 cm) are also being developed. Salpiglossis was once only suitable for growing as a pot plant, but the hybrids can be cultivated outdoors in sheltered sunny places where they will do well, even in poor soil.

Hybrids of the monkey flower, or mimulus, produce larger flowers than those of the wild genus. The tubular blooms, with velvety petals spotted at the flower throat, now come in a range of reds, oranges, yellows, and bicolors. The parent species grows in Chilean bogs, and the hybrids retain a trace of this characteristic, for they prefer moist areas.

However, they are versatile enough to be successfully grown in window boxes or small gardens on the shady side of a building.

By contrast, the gaillardia will survive both heat and drought with equanimity. The uncultivated plant bears a single, rather untidy flower that was not always welcome in the garden. However, there are now double-flowering hybrids that are much neater, and also extend the native color range of the bloom that traditionally has yellow-edged petals of deep red. The gaillardia will thrive best in rich soil, and it needs to be staked and cut back frequently to stay at its best.

GARDEN STYLE GUIDE

Grow mimulus with marigolds or zinnias for a truly warm look. Neither salpiglossis nor gaillardia will be lost in the cheerful crowd of the annual bed. The delicate texture of salpiglossis is best displayed against a gray-foliaged plant near the front of the border.

THE MIMULUS 'YELLOW VELVET' (above) is typical of the rich color this flower brings to cool and shady corners.

THE NEW GAILLARDIA HYBRIDS come in monotones of clear reds or yellows, or, as in the 'Double Mixed' (left), the colors are subtly blended together. These double hybrids are more manageable and much prettier than those of the parent species.

THE GLORIOUS MIX OF burgundy, mauve, pink, cream, and bronze that the botanists have developed in salpiglossis is displayed in this collection of 'Casino Mixed' (right).

48

ORNAMENTAL KALE

The kale plant, botanically a variant of *Brassica oleracea*, has long been grown as a hardy and highly nutritious green in the vegetable garden. But now the ornamental kale, or borecole, brings a bizarre variation of shape to the annual bed.

The ornamental kale's profusion of erect, frilled leaves forms a decorative cone of green mingled with pink, purple, white, or cream tones. Their hybrid vigor makes them easy plants to grow, and they can be treated as hardy annuals.

Sow seeds outdoors in February to March for summer "blooming" or June to July for fall "blooming." Transplant to their final positions once young plants are well established.

Although it will tolerate frost, the ornamental kale does not appreciate very hot weather and usually grows better when planted for a display of superb and unusual color in the fall. All varieties will need a position out of full sun, and shade must be provided in hot areas or on exposed patios. The biggest of the new varieties can be expected to grow to about 20 inches (50 cm) in height.

GARDEN STYLE GUIDE

The curious bulk of long, curly leaves characteristic of the ornamental kale need not be overdominant when plants are incorporated into the border. Blend this foliage into the immediate environment and surround it with pinks and mauves. Or make a splendidly bold arrangement of ornamental kale plants by setting them en masse in a long window box, or individually, or in small groups in a good-sized container on the patio.

The ornamental kale, though not edible, could also be used to provide visual interest in the vegetable garden or to edge a collection of herbs.

ORNAMENTAL KALE WILL complement both delicate foliage and flowers that do justice to its own rich colors. The kale is probably at its most decorative in such a situation (right).

THE ORNAMENTAL KALE SHOWN IN detail is of darker hue and less flamboyant than some of the other new hybrids, yet it still makes an unusual statement in the late summer garden.

PANSIES

The most common garden *Viola*, or pansy, is really itself a hybrid, *Viola × wittrockiana*, and from it many more pansy hybrids have been derived. Botanically, the pansy is a perennial, but the latest hybrids have been bred for bedding and are treated as annuals.

More refinements have ensured that the pansy has a high tolerance of poor weather and is more vigorous than its predecessors, most significantly with a genetic resistance to wilt. Pansies grow best in cool weather and are wonderful in spring gardens.

The great popularity of the pansy, with its demure and velvety face, has inspired botanists to experiment with both the color and the size of the bloom, and there are now wide variations of both, including a pure white and a near-black flower. Start indoors and plant out in early spring. In mild areas sow outdoors in late summer or fall for early spring bloom.

VIOLA TRICOLOR *(ABOVE)*, *'Johnny jump-up,' is the species from which most* Viola × wittrockiana *hybrids are derived. This forgotten parent* has now been revived and is back in cultivation. The small flowers, in three colors as their name suggests, are borne in great profusion.

'JOLLY JOKER' (RIGHT) presents a bold, sharp orange face surrounded by purple. This psychedelic arrangement is one of the many exciting color combinations now being bred in violas. The shock of the colors, which may not appeal to all tastes, is softened by the velvety petals.

A GATHERING OF BLACK BLOOMS, each dotted sharply with a yellow eye, reinforces the special quality of the hybrid viola – it is one of the few flowers that can be persuaded to produce such dark petals. This hybrid is named 'Molly Sanderson'.

ASTERS

Annual aster hybrids are derived from *Callistephus chinensis*, the China aster. These daisy-like flowers, which prefer a well-drained soil and sunny position, are problematical to grow because of aster wilt, for which there is no treatment. The disease can affect plants at any stage, from the seedlings onward. However, the breeders have done — and, indeed, are still doing — much research into producing varieties that are resistant to this disease, and to mildew, which has also beset the older forms.

The China aster comes in many hybrid forms — tall, dwarf, single, double — and in a color range of white, pink, crimson, and purple. Flowers have been bred to have the fluffy form of powder puffs or to bear thin, spiky petals that give a cactus-like look. Blooms of all types are long lasting in cut-flower arrangements and are prized for this trait.

Annual asters bloom from July until the first frosts of fall. Seeds may be sown outdoors in April or May, or started in a heated tray for propagating two months earlier than this. They are at their best when used as edging or as massed bedding subjects.

A STRONG COLOR COMBINATION of powerful red surrounding a white center moves the China aster 'Gusford Supreme' (above) away from the usual gentle hues of this popular summer annual.

THE DWARF COMET SERIES OF China asters (left) has beautifully formed fluffy flowers and is a welcome addition to the rock garden.

ELEGANT, SPIKY PETALS IN traditional pink are found in the hybrid Callistephus chinensis 'Rose' (right).

HERBACEOUS PERENNIALS

The colorful herbaceous perennials have long been garden favorites, not least because they require less care and maintenance than the short-lived annuals. But many herbaceous perennials have, by nature, invasive habits and quickly spread themselves across the border. The newer hybrids have been bred either to eliminate these wandering ways or, at least, to inhibit them. Plants with compact or restricted habits have been introduced, bringing a more orderly note to the herbaceous border.

The great height of some perennials means that they stood awkward and overpowering in small city gardens. Shorter, stockier versions of many of these tall plants have thus evolved as a result of the breeders' efforts.

Not all the breeding of herbaceous perennials has been motivated by considerations of the mundane practicalities of gardening. The flowers, too, have been boldly developed, and these experiments have borne results in the form of larger blooms and unusual colors. Ambitious projects to create hues that nature withheld from the perennial palette have achieved success in breeding programs such as the one which, after many years of intensive effort, has finally produced a true red delphinium.

The intended use of many of the new hybrids is reflected in garden design trends. Now herbaceous perennials are used in mixed borders with deciduous and evergreen shrubs, creating a greater variety and depth.

New, bright blooms confirm all expectations in a trial bed of compact perennial Charm chrysanthemums for eventual use in the herbaceous border.

CROCOSMIAS

These brilliant members of the iris family are native to South Africa. Although they grow from small corms, they are usually treated in the garden as herbaceous perennials. In the last century, a French family, the Lemoines of Nancy, started to experiment and produced a hybrid *Crocosmia x crocosmiiflora*, known as "montbretia." This started a trend, and today there are many fine hybrids available from nurseries and suppliers.

Crocosmias typically form dense clumps of swordlike leaves, and were once invasive, spreading plants. In the newest hybrids this tiresome trait is inhibited. Breeding has also created bright new blooms in a variety of less strident colors with subtle changes in form.

The flowers are often preferred when cut for vase arrangements, but the crocosmia has long been part of the cottage-style design, and gardeners warmly welcome the latest additions. It will thrive in any well-drained soil and tolerate all but the most severe winter weather. Blooming is from July through to September.

THE APPROPRIATE VARIETAL name 'Solfataire' (above) reflects the sharply acid yellow of this hybrid's smooth petals which contrast perfectly with the bronze green sword-shaped leaves. This was one of the first of the new crocosmias.

THE DELICATE ARCH OF THE flowerhead, leaning into erect leaves, gives 'Jenny Bloom' (right) a fine graceful form. The blooms of this hybrid make excellent cut flowers. This crocosmia will reach about 36 inches (90 cm) in height. Northern gardeners must dig the bulbs in fall and store them indoors over winter.

'Lucifer' (left) is characterized by clusters of red hot blooms hanging on a long length of stem. The arrangement of open flowers making way for closed buds beyond provides an attractive growth pattern.

GARDEN STYLE GUIDE

The graceful curve of the stalks and the vivid flowers are best displayed when crocosmia is grown in clumps. Alternatively, enhance the bright yellow blooms of new varieties by growing them near the blues of a ceanothus.

POPPIES

The perennial *Papaver orientale*, or oriental poppy, is the most conspicuous of all the members of this popular genus. And it has been bred to such a gorgeous brilliance that it can be used in gardens of formal sophistication, and in simple cottage and free country arrangements.

The poppy's great papery bloom is carried high above coarse, hairy leaves. The long stalks generally need staking, but hybrids are being developed that have strong and sturdy stems that can stand on their own. However, most of the genetic experiments have concentrated on ever more enormous blooms, some of which now reach 8 inches (20 cm) across. Parallel research has given the wide, papery petals more substance than previously, which makes them able to withstand bad weather.

The poppy was originally red, and this is still a favorite hue, but the new plants flower in combinations of pink and white and often bear a semidouble bloom. The oriental poppy is one of the hardiest of herbaceous perennials. Start indoors from seed, or propagate new plants by division. In mild areas, regular deadheading will encourage a second flowering later in the season. Plants can be propagated by dividing clumps in spring and cuttings usually take with ease.

GARDEN STYLE GUIDE

When the splendid flowering is over, the *Papaver orientale* flower shrivels and the coarse foliage dies. Its position must thus be given careful thought so that the resulting unsightly gaps it leaves can be covered or made unobtrusive. The cloudy floating foliage and blossom of gypsophila help to obscure the poppy's dying leaves. *Lathyrus latifolius* 'Alba' and helenium are also good neighbors.

It is still worth planning to accommodate this less than pleasing trait, for the splendor of the flower is a highlight of the perennial garden. The attractive hairy pepperpot seed heads can be kept for dry arrangements.

THE ORIGINAL RED IS RETAINED IN 'Curlilocks' (left), but the petals have a "shredded" edge, resulting in a spiky appearance quite unexpected in the oriental poppy.

'MARCUS PERRY' (RIGHT) IS A marvelous example of the hybrid color range. It has retained the traditional bowl-shaped flower and has kept the strange allure of the wide, papery petals pinned to a deep, dark center.

KNIPHOFIAS AND AGAPANTHUS

With their unusual shapes and pleasing colors, both *Kniphofia* and *Agapanthus* are traditional herbaceous border plants bred in new varieties guaranteed to bring flair and style to the garden.

Kniphofia is a warmth-loving native of Africa, and the hybrids have been bred to produce a much hardier plant than the species and a more subtle range of colors than the original scarlet. Plants need full sun in temperate climates but will thrive in most garden soils. In colder situations, their leaves should be tied up in a bunch during winter with straw or leaf cover mounded around the plant. They dislike being transplanted, although older plants can be lifted and divided in spring.

There are many hybrids of agapanthus, the African lily, featuring shades of blue and purple in the flowers and gray and bluish tones in the leaves. The latest hybrids have been bred to be frost hardy, but prefer a sunny position and the benefits of well-drained soil. Agapanthus are often grown in tubs and brought indoors for the winter. Agapanthus flowers from July through to September. The blooms can be successfully dried for indoor arrangements.

New varieties of kniphofia and agapanthus are best purchased as ready-grown plants, since they are very slow growing from seed. Both will reach a height of nearly 36 inches (90 cm), although there are dwarf varieties of the kniphofia that grow to only 12 inches (30 cm). The biggest of the hybrid blooms are racemes that may measure 10 inches (25 cm) or more in length overall and each may bear more than 100 tubular flowers.

THE KNIPHOFIA (LEFT) IS commonly known as the red hot poker, but the lovely lemon and cream tones of this subtle yellow hybrid 'Maid of Orleans' belie its traditional title.

A gathering of agapanthus plants can become the center of attraction in the garden. Here the hybrid 'Dorothy Parker' dazzles the eye with an intense violet blue.

GARDEN STYLE GUIDE

Both kniphofia and agapanthus can be grown on their own as focal points in the border, but the blues and purples of the agapanthus will be emphasized if plants are combined with the gray foliage of lavender and artemesia. Grow the kniphofia against alchemillas and hemerocallis for a similar complementary effect.

IRISES

The beauty of the *Iris* has long been appreciated by artists and gardeners alike, but it is the scientists who have coaxed and nurtured hybrids to emphasize the unique aesthetic values of this flower. Its architectural form has been developed to create blooms of magnificent scale and shape, held high on elegant, erect stems.

Of the thousand or more species of iris, the geneticists and gardeners have favored the development of the Bearded irises (classified as Tall, Intermediate, or Dwarf, depending on their height), which grow from rhizomes. Much of the inspiration for this research came from the American, A.H. Sturtevant, and his work done early this century. As a result, not only has the bold outline of the flower been highlighted, but the wonderful diversity of color within the genus has also been exploited.

Most Bearded types will adapt to a wide range of conditions, but the Tall Bearded will not tolerate being crowded by other plants, and thrives only in well-prepared, well-drained soil. But, given space and sun, most allow the gardener a careless disregard for color planning, since any combination of hues and tones will create a gorgeous display.

GARDEN STYLE GUIDE

All types of Bearded irises can be included in a massed border and can be grown with a wide variety of annuals and perennials. Their bold form is most flamboyantly displayed when the plants are grown in sizeable clumps. Choose colors to produce a shaded effect across a mass of planting in a large border. These irises also look effective when placed against a backdrop of subtle gray or muted foliage, or when scattered to bloom among the later daffodils and early varieties of tulips.

THE TRADITIONAL HERALDIC outline is softened in this Tall Bearded 'Dancer's Veil' (above). It needs to be carefully positioned in the garden if its subtlety is to be fully appreciated.

'RASPBERRY BLUSH' (RIGHT), A new and unusual iris color, has petals held in a wide, carefree manner.

'BOLD PRINT' (FAR LEFT) IS AN Intermediate Bearded aptly named for its crisp, clear, and sharp markings.

THE BEARD CREATES A SMUDGED effect across the deep, dark shades of 'Llanthony' (left).

IRISES

The iris was named for the Greek rainbow goddess, and science has widened the range and combination of hues to create blooms of deepest velvet blue, pale gold and pastel pink, of rich, creamy browns, lemon yellows, and near-whites.

Tall Bearded irises grow from 30 to 60 inches (75 to 150 cm) with flowers up to 6 inches (15 cm) or more across. The tallest of these plants are of such a bold scale, and the new hybrids so outstanding in color and line, that many gardeners prefer to show them off in their own bed. Placed against a clipped yew hedge or a stone wall, they will make a glorious display. The flowering season is for a few weeks in April, May, or June, depending upon the variety.

The Intermediate Beardeds range from 10 to 36 inches (25 to 90 cm) in height, with flowers up to 5 inches (12 cm) across. Dwarf Beardeds are from 9 to 12 inches (22 to 30 cm) tall with 4-inch (10-cm) flowers. Site single clumps of irises against a gate or near the kitchen door where they can best be seen and appreciated. Rhizomes should be planted or divided and moved before the middle of August, and set in the ground so that their tops are exposed to the sun, not covered by soil.

BROWN IS A COLOR MUCH favored by the breeders of the Tall Bearded. Here, in 'Isabella Hunter', which grows to 50 inches (1.25 m) and flowers in midsummer, petals in spun gold and white are delicately veined in brown to make a spectacularly decorative garden plant.

This iris shows to perfection the arrangement of the petals in the bloom. The three erect inner petals are the "standards." The three outer drooping petals are the "falls." The falls bear the fleshy hairs or "beard," which in this instance are a vibrant shades of orange.

'LIGHT LAUGHTER' (LEFT) HAS A delicacy and softness not usually found in the strong tones of the iris. The breeder has given this bloom subtle cream and mushroom shades in its petals.

AN EXTRAORDINARY combination of the traditional purples and yellows of the iris is found in the shades of 'Brown Lasso', while the shape has been endowed with art nouveau lines and curves.

BREEDERS OF IRISES PAY MUCH attention to the color and quality of the beard. In 'Sarah Taylor' (above), a spring-flowering Intermediate Bearded, the beard is a deep lilac adorning the pale yellows and creams of the fall petals. The standards have delicately waved edges.

AQUILEGIAS AND HOLLYHOCKS

Both the columbine *Aquilegia* and the hollyhock *Althaea (Alcea)* are by nature tall plants – indeed the hollyhock is the most majestic of perennials. Genetic experimentation has been used on both these genera, to make them even taller or to make them shorter and more compact.

The hollyhock now comes in dwarf varieties with double blooms. Short-lived perennials often treated as biennials, some hybrids have been grown to behave as annuals, and many are bred to be less vulnerable to rust than the original plants were.

Breeders have worked to make the columbine a more robust plant, able to withstand attack by wind. In some varieties, their fernlike foliage has been deepened from a light to a stronger green and, of course, genetics now dictates the length of the delicate spurs that decorate each of the five petals of the flower. The color ranges of these blooms have also been widened to create a greater choice of pinks, purples, reds, creams, and yellows.

GARDEN STYLE GUIDE

The tall hollyhocks are obvious candidates to place against garden walls or stand sentry at the back of the border. The dwarf varieties make a lovely massed summer bedding.

The dainty spurred columbine should be included in every flower border, and can be placed near *Salvia farinacea* 'Victoria', *Campanula*, and *Hemerocallis citrina*. Columbine makes a suitable partner for most other perennials.

AN EARLY HYBRID OF THE columbine is 'Nora Barlow' (above left), which has recently been revived. The soft, fluffy blossom, with its slightly droopy air, is increasingly popular. It looks particularly pleasing grown en masse to bloom in late spring and early summer, but prefers cool positions.

McKana's Giant (above) is among the best of all the Aquilegia hybrids. It can grow to a height of 36 inches (90 cm), and the spurs are long and prominent.

THIS DWARF VARIETY OF THE hollyhock 'Majorette' (right) is only 24 inches (60 cm) tall.

CONEFLOWERS

The *Rudbeckia*, also known as the coneflower or gloriosa daisy, is a hardy native of North America. Until recently, its chief disadvantage in the garden has been that, like the natural species, it tends to be spindly and weedlike in habit. However, the breeding of the hybrid *Rudbeckia fulgida* 'Goldsturm' has created plants of vigorous, controlled growth far superior to the old versions, and these are worthy additions to the herbaceous border.

Even in poor soil, and in sun or shade, these new rudbeckias will survive for years, and they are remarkably resistant to attack by insects and disease. They have fine, bright blooms and a compact branching habit, and make a good display against walls or wherever a dash of permanent summer color is required. Large plants can be easily propagated in spring by division.

The closely related *Ratibida* is also a native of North America, where it is commonly known as the prairie coneflower. It is a new introduction to the gardens of Europe, but its distinctive bloom and hardy nature are qualities that will attract those gardeners in search of the unusual – but not difficult – plant with which to embellish their herbaceous borders. It has a coarse and hairy foliage that is not unattractive in a wild way and that gives a hint of the plant's useful capacity to withstand dry soils and lack of regular water.

THE RUDBECKIA *'GOLDSTURM' (left) is a gardener's dream. It is ideal for the summer border, where it will bloom continuously, supplying color well into fall.*
Fresh blooms will overlap dying ones, but since these flowers are excellent in cut arrangements, there should rarely be any old heads.

THE RATIBIDA (RIGHT) BEARS ITS strange, solitary heads on long, separate flower stalks. The odd receptacle in its center has earned it, with the rudbeckia, the familiar name of coneflower. This plant deserves a granite wall or other pale background to enhance its unusual beauty.

PRIMULAS

Primulas are members of a large family of plants that includes primroses, polyanthus, and auriculas. Not only are the species numerous, but so are the hybrids that include many once-tender subjects that will now grow outdoors.

The hybrids are so charming and colorful that the urge to produce new, bizarre color strains is irresistible to even the most amateur botanist. Indeed, many nurseries cherish their own strains of primula. Doubles, bicolors, and multicolors, new shades, and ever-larger blooms are among the successful range of new primroses, auriculas, and polyanthus. These hybrids flower from May to June. They are somewhat difficult to grow in the U.S. and are best for the Pacific Northwest.

EXCITING AND EXTRAORDINARY color combinations have been produced in Primula auricula 'Stubb's Tartan' *(right) and* 'Valerie' *(below). Both these examples reveal the fascination of work being done on the primula to breed ever more unusual designs to delight the eye.*

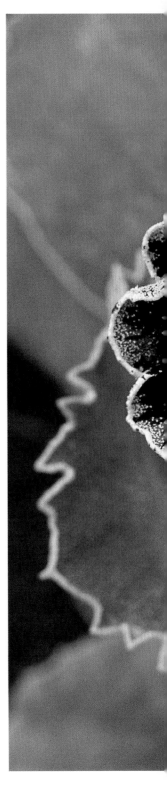

'PACIFIC GIANTS MIXED' (LEFT) are long flowering with large blooms of rich, sharp color. The flowers are held on stout stems about 12 inches (30 cm) high, and the corrugated leaves form a subtle green frame to the brightness of the blooms.

GARDEN STYLE GUIDE

Their low-growing habit and preference for moist soil make hybrid polyanthus, primulas, and auriculas well suited to sheltered banks, and they will tolerate partial shade. Allow them to gather in odd corners or shelter under shrubs, skirt pathways, or fill a small bed of their own. They will blend happily with spring bulbs, can be used in formal designs, and are cheerfully decorative in pots or window boxes. In any situation the foliage forms a pleasing rosette.

The *Achillea* is a wonderfully drought-resistant perennial that will survive in the poorest soil. Indeed, several varieties are regarded as rank weeds in some areas. However, hybridization of a range of species, including *A. millefolium*, *A. filipendulina*, and *A. tomentosa* has produced some splendid plants of controlled growth. These are now available to gardeners in a wide variety of single and mixed colors ranging from salmon pink to deep red, and have contributed toward making achillea justifiably popular among flower gardeners. As well as strong color, the curious shape of achillea's multiflowered heads brings diversity of form to the border. Their use also extends beyond the flowerbed, for they make an excellent dried arrangement.

Sow the seeds in the open in early spring and provide plants with a permanent position in full sun. Annual division of the clumps will increase the growth of the achillea, and it can also be propagated by means of cuttings. Although the plant can reach a height of 54 inches (1.4 m), it needs staking only if it has been placed in an exposed site. The flowers of the new hybrids, like the old forms, have a distinctive "musty" odor.

IN THE NATIVE ACHILLEA, YELLOW and white are the only pure flower colors. The hybrid named 'The Beacon' (left) has been created in an unusual clear cerise, which is particularly attractive presented in the circular clusters of small flowers so characteristic of the species Achillea filipendulina *from which the hybrid was bred.*

MANY GARDEN COLOR SCHEMES will benefit from the addition of a touch of pastel or white. The graceful clusters of the new achillea 'Great Expectations' are designed to create exactly this lightening effect in the garden.

GARDEN STYLE GUIDE

The achillea is suited to middle-distance planting. It will look good with most of its neighbors in the herbaceous border or bed, where its ferny foliage will intermingle softly with a variety of greenery.

Place it with eryngium for a particularly graceful effect. The tallest of the new varieties may need staking. If so, make sure that the supports or sticks are as unobtrusive as possible.

PEONIES

The herbaceous peony, *Paeonia*, can be described botanically as a bushy, decorative perennial. This is an accurate but inadequate description of a true garden beauty.

The garden peony is not only a royal presence in the border, but is also hardy, dependable, easy to grow and very long living. The plant is also adored for its compelling fragrance. It should be planted with its crown less than 2 inches (5 cm) from the surface in a slightly acid, well-drained soil; keep animal manure or chemical fertilizer away from it.

The species *P. lactiflora*, from which most hybrids are bred, is smaller in height and blossom size than any of its glorious progeny – and there are many hybrids in pinks, reds, and whites.

'BOWL OF BEAUTY' (RIGHT) HAS wide, shell-shaped petals holding an inner froth of narrow petaloids. This design lends itself to the development of a bicolored bloom, and this is a splendid example of such breeding.

THE RICH, RED BLOOMS OF Paeonia lactiflora 'Cherry' (above) lift their decorative heads on elegant stems. When the blossom fades, the neat foliage remains green and lustrous to give depth to other summer flowers. As a cut flower the peony's glamour will last in the vase for many days before fading.

'MONSIEUR JULES ELIE' (RIGHT) is one of the best double hybrids. It is bred to be very free flowering, blooming from May to July, whereas many other peonies fade in June. The many-petalled blooms can reach 7 inches (18 cm) across. Plants form dense, compact clumps endowed with vigorous foliage.

GARDEN STYLE GUIDE

The American Peony Society recognizes five types within *P. lactiflora* – Chinese, Japanese, anemone, semi-double, and double – but nurseries tend to use looser descriptions based on shape or color. Whichever type is chosen it must be sited with care, since all of them hate to be moved.

Line a path with peonies and plant catmint in front of them, or group them among *Stachys macrantha* 'Rosea' or 'Violacea'. The herbaceous border is also a good place for peonies, and here their strong foliage is best appreciated when placed in the middle of the border.

DELPHINIUMS

Endowed with majestic beauty, delphiniums also have an endearing quality that gives them universal appeal. The silhouettes of the tall spires bring a grand aspect to any part of the garden, but this superiority is softened by the pure colors of the dense flowerheads.

Some of the many hybrids, mainly those known as the Wrexham Strain, can reach 72 inches (1.8 m) in height, and the Giant Pacific Hybrids carry florets nearly 6 inches (15 cm) across. Floret shapes and styles vary widely, and hybrid colors range from true blue – a rare hue in the garden – through mauve, white, pink, and now, after years of effort, even red.

They are difficult to grow in the U.S., especially in hot regions. Plant in rich, slightly alkaline soil in an open area. Stake heavy flower spikes.

THE SLIGHTLY CRUMPLED AIR OF the new delphinium 'Clifford Lass' (above) is matched by the coppery shadows held within the gentle mauve of the standard-shaped flower. Mix it with delphiniums of other shades to create a subtle effect in a sunny part of the herbaceous border.

THE BOTANIST'S DREAM COME true – a very red, very warm 'Pink Delphinium' (right) carries its dazzling color in tightly packed florets. These red delphiniums are not yet readily available to gardeners, but work continues apace to create varieties suitable for average garden conditions.

THE WONDERFUL WHITE delphinium has an air of purity and majesty that would enrich any herbaceous border. The creamy unified florets present a controlled, statuesque display in the hybrid 'Butterball' (top left).

THESE LOOSE, FLUFFY BLOOMS have the appropriate name of 'Can Can' (left). The frilled and delicate blossom – infinitely more subtle than the lesser-bred blues of average delphiniums – suggests the lace and frippery of the Parisian dancing girls.

HOSTAS AND EUPHORBIAS

Both the *Hosta* and the *Euphorbia* are flower garden plants prized for their foliage and also for their adaptability, which makes them easy to maintain.

The hosta has a splendid, rhythmic quality that the breeders have exploited by extending or swirling the natural flow of the large, shapely leaves. They have furled the edges of these leaves, or enlarged them into sculptural, broad forms and have made them dusky blue in tone, or bold green variegated with white or cream markings. The hosta flowers, though less significant than the leaves, have also drawn the attention of the breeders.

Eurphorbia marginata forms an attractive mound of foliage, with leaves bearing broad margins of pale colors. These margins have been altered to be broad or narrow, cream or white. The geneticists have also produced varieties of this plant that can be treated as annuals and used in bedding designs.

GARDEN STYLE GUIDE

The hosta has the confidence of a natural town dweller, gracing urban gardens with its foliage, but it will adorn any garden as ground cover under trees, in a border, or near a pool. *Euphorbia marginata* is best suited to the rock garden or the front of a bed or border.

A BED OF MIXED HOSTAS (FAR left) reveals the rich textural quality and variegated color that have been produced by the breeders of this plant. 'August Moon' (above) typifies the development of pale, bright leaves and tall racemes of scented blooms.

IN EUPHORBIA MARGINATA 'Berg Kristall' (left), the pale margins are narrowed to a mere outline on the leaves, but extended widely on the flower.

ROSES

Modern rose breeding freely explores all possible combinations in its search for new color and shape, for improved hardiness, disease-resistance, and a wider range of growth habits. And because rose lovers seek out the legendary scent of this flower, attempts are made to retain or extend the range of perfumes.

As a result of recent activity, not only have hundreds of new varieties been produced, but the old definitions of Hybrid Tea and Floribunda are becoming increasingly untenable. Complex interbreeding between these two groups means that they are now often classed as Large-flowered and Cluster-flowered roses.

In Shrub roses, the choice of new varieties now spans Modern Shrub roses, which are like big versions of the old Floribundas, and New English roses, which have the appearance of a Shrub rose, but are more manageable. Also significant in the burgeoning of new roses is that the plants are now being increased by means of "micropropagation" (see page 8).

Other trends in rose growing reflect new needs in the garden. Ground-cover and minia-ture roses have experienced a particular surge in popularity. Rose blooms can range from a single collection of petals to complex arrangements containing nearly 100 petals. Color choice, too, is ever wider. But while it is possible to grow a rose that is purple or even orange brown, the quest for the true blue rose continues.

NEW VARIETIES OF PROSTRATE ROSES MAKE A MAGNIFICENT ground cover. Here 'Pink Bells' and 'Snow Carpet' form the background and foreground, respectively.

82

PATIO ROSES

Over the last 50 years hybrid roses have increased in popularity. The newest trends in rose breeding have been led by a demand from hundreds of city gardeners whose horticultural activities are confined by lack of space. The result is a hybrid "patio" rose bush that has become short and compact but that retains the full bloom size of its original parent.

These patio roses have been created by crosses between roses of small stature and outstanding blooms including species, Large-flowered, Cluster-flowered, and miniatures. Despite a faltering start, during which many hybrids proved to be lacking in vigor and were susceptible to disease, the patio roses now on the market are comparatively hardy and less vulnerable than before to black spot, mildew, and rust.

Plant out patio roses in their dormant period between fall and spring. If bought in "micro-prop" form (see p. 86), and thus grown on their own roots, they should be planted with the lowest branches level with the soil. If budded onto a rootstock, they should be planted with the budding union about an inch (2.5 cm) below ground level.

GARDEN STYLE GUIDE

The new short or "patio" rose is designed to grow as a low bush with a rich flower value, and it reaches a height of only 24 inches (60 cm). Its small habit means that it can be grown in ornamental urns, in paving spaces, and used to edge beds and borders. And, as its name implies, it is ideally suited to being cultivated on the patio.

The great virtue of these roses is that their blooms are often large and numerous, so that they can bring color and texture to a small space. Mass them in a window box or a small bed, or plant one in its own pot. This is the ideal rose for those rose lovers with only a ledge or container for a garden.

'ANNA FORD' (LEFT) CARRIES scores of bright mandarin-colored blooms surrounded by small, shiny leaves. It is a delightful edging plant, or can be used to make a petite hedging in a small but carefully landscaped garden.

IT IS RARE IN MODERN HYBRIDS, and even more so in a patio rose, to see the old-fashioned quarter bloom produced by 'Rosabell' (left). These traditional flowers are borne on a bush of a mere 15 inches (38 cm).

THE LOVELY, LIMPID BLOOM OF 'Gentle Touch' (above) imitates the form of a Large-flowered rose. The flowers grow in soft clusters, large in proportion to the plant size, and bring a mass of color to a small garden.

CLUSTER-FLOWERED ROSES

The many varieties bred within the ever popular Cluster-flowered (Floribunda) hybrids produce single, semi-double, and fully double blooms. They often flower continuously all summer long and even into fall. These hybrids do not require disbudding, but the entire truss should be removed after flowering to encourage new blooms.

Cluster-flowered roses vary in height from 20 to 60 inches (50 to 150 cm) and some bear blooms that are 4 inches (10 cm) across, but many are scentless or only weakly fragrant. Colors among the new hybrids are wide ranging and include unusual subtle shades and some eye-catching combinations.

'EYEPAINT' (ABOVE) WAS THE first of the "handpainted" roses to be widely available. From it the breeders have created a range of startling effects in bright colors. Use these roses in bold garden designs or to create a sharp accent among flowers and foliage of subtle hues. 'Drummer Boy' (left) has a delicate fragrance and flowers quickly and freely. It reaches a height of 24 inches (60 cm) and allowance should be made for this rose's natural tendency to spread.

'GREENSLEEVES' (LEFT) BRINGS an unusual subtlety to the much-loved white rose. A slight and delicate shadow of green fills the depths of the softly furled petals. The buds are pink, and it is at this stage that the rose should be cut. The clusters will open over several days, so gradually revealing the delicate chartreuse green hue of the interior of each bloom.

THE DOUBLE BLOSSOM OF PALE dusk colors in 'Nimbus' (below) is supported on a strong plant with good, clear foliage. It attains a height of 24 inches (60 cm) and flowers from July to September. 'Jocelyn' (left) has deep green, polished foliage with a distinctive crinkled edge. The bloom deepens in color to a bruised mauve as it ages.

THE FREE-FLOWERING 'Brown Velvet' (above) has a strange red tone which verges on brown, a new color in roses. It is a strong growing plant, reaching 36 inches (90 cm), and makes a good cut flower. A powerful scent, rare in the Cluster-flowered roses, is one of the delights of 'Champagne Cocktail' (left), a vigorous plant of bushy well shaped habit.

HYBRID TEA ROSES

Rose breeders are held by the beauty of the Hybrid Teas (also called Large-flowered roses), and much research is being directed toward developing rich, complex flower forms, a greater range of colors, and an ever more delicious fragrance.

The most notable practical result of the geneticists' efforts is that these roses have been revived as permanent bedding plants, for they have bred a modern plant that is vigorous and hardy. The Large-flowered rose is tolerant of most soils and situations, more resistant to disease, and has a continuity of flower not equaled in any other garden plant. With these roses – supreme examples of the breeders' art – the difficulties that exasperated our grandparents have been eliminated for good.

'SILVER JUBILEE' (BELOW) IS THE best Hybrid Tea rose to be bred in recent years and has been a parent for many new hybrids. The blooms have a weak fragrance.

WITH A VIGOROUS BRANCHING habit, 'Polar Star' (right) is a high-centered, rare white rose. Breeders have striven to remove traces of yellow or pink from such blooms.

GARDEN STYLE GUIDE

It is traditional to grow roses in their own beds, and to keep the different types separate. However, the Hybrid Tea roses will keep good company with nemophila, godetia, and alyssum, or can be mixed with herbaceous perennials in a border setting.

Underplanted violas or an edging of dianthus will also make pleasing neighbors.

Make sure that these roses are not planted under or near trees, which will deprive them of nutrients, and provide them with well-drained soil in a sunny position.

A TRIUMPHANT NEW DEPTH OF color has been introduced to the rose collection with 'Big Purple' (above). The flowers, which are derived from a shade of maroon, have a strong fragrance and are surrounded by dark, mat foliage on a medium-sized bush. The breeders are justly proud of the strength of color they have created in this Hybrid Tea rose.

'SUNSET SONG' (RIGHT) IS AN original combination of amber rose blooms and bronze-hued foliage.

THE HYBRID TEA 'DOUBLE Delight' (overleaf) is a small rose, the most unusual hybrid of the last decade. It has been endowed with an entirely new color combination and an intense scent.

MODERN HYBRID SHRUB ROSES

These shrub roses are mostly Cluster-flowered forms similar to the old Floribundas. They have been developed from a fascinating mix of hybrids created by crossing species from all over the world, and they retain a charming "old-fashioned" appearance. The Modern English types are a variant of them.

These roses can grow into magnificent shrubs that require trimming rather than pruning and demand minimal maintenance, being disease-resistant and scornful of pests. The Modern Shrub rose is free-flowering, producing blooms of quality either singly or in sprays, and many also have an excellent glistening foliage. Some have a lax habit and can be successfully trained to grow up poles. This rose is a suitable plant for most gardens.

'PAM AYRES' (ABOVE) IS A FREE-flowering, vigorous rose with an unexpected bonus for the gardener. As it matures, the bloom changes from a vivid yellow to scarlet.

IN 'ABRAHAM DARBY' (LEFT) THE breeder has created a glorious golden pink bloom. This versatile Modern English Shrub rose can be trained and used as a small hedge.

'ENGLISH GARDEN' (RIGHT) HAS the soft, unstructured appeal of an old cottage rose but is much easier to cultivate than the species roses. This hardy new hybrid displays all the advantages of modern breeding.

MODERN ENGLISH SHRUB ROSES

Modern English Shrub roses combine the habits of a shrub rose with the flowering qualities of the Cluster-flowered, or Floribunda, rose. Thus the Modern English Shrub rose, an exciting development in the long story of rose cultivation, has the ease of growth, hardiness, and vigor of the Cluster-flowered rose but, like this parent, also lacks fragrance.

The outstanding characteristic of the Modern English Shrub roses are their fully double, often quartered blooms, which imitate the old-fashioned roses but have greater size and style on plants of a more orderly habit.

These roses are easy to grow but like other roses need to be fed regularly if they are to thrive. They do not require heavy pruning; indeed strong, young growth should be allowed to develop, since this helps to promote a good shape. Position plants so that the sun reaches their bases.

GARDEN STYLE GUIDE

All Shrub roses, including the Modern English types, with their luxurious foliage and bushy shape, are ideal specimen plants, but the gardener should plan to take advantage of their informal looks. Shrub roses can also be used for hedging or in the herbaceous border.

'MARY ROSE' (TOP RIGHT) IS A branching, spreading plant and the blooms are a good size. This rose could be grown as ground cover.

'ST. CECILIA' (RIGHT) IS A Modern English Shrub rose that would be superb as a hedge. The cream pink flowers against clear green foliage will suit any color scheme.

'HERITAGE' (LEFT) IS A MODERN English Shrub with a perfectly quartered bloom. The golden buds open to display the pink and cream petals.

THIS MODERN ENGLISH BLOOM (above) bears the proud name of the Bard, 'William Shakespeare'. It is typified by a vigorous, branching habit and glossy foliage.

MINIATURE AND PROSTRATE ROSES

Miniature roses, which have recently burgeoned in popularity among rose breeders and growers, have inherited from their Chinese ancestors a long flowering season and an appealing form. The group divides into two sections; those that grow from 9 to 12 inches (23 to 30 cm) and larger types that grow to 15 inches (40 cm). The taller forms are suitable for being trained as standards.

Both types of miniatures bear semidouble or double flowers, usually ¾ to 1 inch (2 to 2.5 cm) across, and have pleasing, but not bright, green foliage. Their stems are virtually thorn-free. Miniature roses are ideal container plants, and can be used as indoor plants for short periods, but they do need spells outdoors if they are to survive.

Hardy deciduous prostrate roses have been developed as ground cover, and the newest hybrids make a splendid display with their spreading, slender stems and free-flowering habit. Not only has the ability to form a dense growth been engineered but, through numerous crosses, a variety of colors has been produced in flowers ranging from singles through to full doubles.

THE MINIATURE 'SNOWBALL' (below) bears fluffy rosettes, set against bright foliage. It is a low and dainty plant that creates a soft, full "cushion." This makes it suitable for edging borders or for creating the effect of a low-growing miniature hedge.

THE EXCELLENT MINIATURE, 'Angela Rippon' (top right) is a substantial plant, bushy and leafy. It has a warm, bright color, is free-flowering, and grows to a height of 18 inches (45 cm). These features make it one of the best new miniatures.

'NOZOMI' (ABOVE) IS A prostrate rose, offering slender stems and tiny leaves with an abundance of blossom. It was a vital forerunner and breeding parent of the wide range of prostrate types available today. The pale blooms are both exquisite and elegant.

BRIGHT FREE-FLOWERING BLOOMS make this prostrate rose a most appealing ground cover. 'Red Bells' (right) will create a brilliant display in an informal garden, falling and spreading over a bank or a flat area. Like many roses of this type, it may be successfully trained as a climber.

GARDEN STYLE GUIDE

Prostrate roses grow in low mounds or they can form extensive mats of flower and foliage. Grow them over a low wall or an old tree trunk. Small banks or hillocks can be covered with these roses, and they make excellent edging plants. They can also be used as dwarf climbers, to reach 60 to 72 inches (1.5 to 1.8 m). Use miniatures en masse in beds, grow them in containers, train them over low garden features, but only grow them in the rock garden if there is assurance of sufficient depth of soil.

BULBS, CORMS, AND TUBERS

Of all the new and exciting flowers that can be grown in the garden, those that propagate themselves from underground organs – bulbs, corms, and tubers – are among the loveliest and the strangest. Narcissi, gladiolas, lilies, tulips, and dahlias are among the ever-popular plants that have held the attention of the breeders.

The notion that the shapes of these flowers could be curled, given rococo furls and twists, or bred in colors ever more subtle in their shading or brilliant in their tone has excited breeders for generations. The modern botanical alchemists experiment to create a pink-trumpeted narcissus, or to deepen the brazen scarlet of the common-place tulip into velvet black. These ambitions may not have been realized yet, but the endless experiments have brought a wonderful choice of hybrid blooms into the bulb market.

Gardeners can now ornament their spring gardens with interesting flower formations and introduce amazing polychrome color. But an equally gratifying result of the breeders' work is that previously rare and unstable bulb species are now within the grasp of all gardeners.

Plants such as the lilies, by nature awkward and resistant to cultivation, are now available in hybrid forms that respond to ordinary garden-care routines. Scientists have also found ways of either making the flowering period begin earlier than in the native species or delaying its start so that the garden can retain its color all year.

THE STIFF, PROUD CUPS OF THE TULIP ARE TRANSFORMED THROUGH hybridization into lax petals of grand size as in the Parrot tulip 'Fluffy' grown here in an informal setting.

TULIPS

Many of today's gardeners want plants that are easy to cultivate, labor free, and visually gorgeous. The tulips, typified by waxy petals, enameled colors, and an architectural form, offer all these qualities, with embellishments produced by the breeders' efforts.

Tulip breeding is now a huge commercial activity, especially in the Netherlands, which exports tulips all over the world. However, not all tulips are produced by deliberate breeding programs: chance can play a part. Not only can tulips produce their own sports, or mutations, but harmless viruses can infect the plant and cause a permanent change in its genetic make-up. The streaking of the petals of Rembrandts is a prime example.

The hundreds of tulips currently available are grouped into 15 horticultural divisions and categorized in two ways. Those classified by flower type include, most importantly, Single Earlies, Double Earlies, Triumphs, Darwin Hybrids, Lily-flowered, Fringed, Viridiflora, Rembrandt, Parrots, and Double Lates. Hybrid tulips – Kaufmanniana, Fosteriana, and Gregii – and species tulips are grouped and named according to their breeding pedigree.

Every year brings new tulip introductions to the market. Flowers that once were rigid and formal have been softened by varieties endowed with frilled petals, made frivolously double, or enhanced with green outer petals. There are tall Fosteriana hybrids with stems up to 18 inches (46 cm) tall and small species less than 5 inches (12.5 cm) high. Black tulips have been created, and true blue is the only color not yet available in the vast spectrum of hues. Flowering time has been extended at both ends of the spring season.

GARDEN STYLE GUIDE

Hybrid tulips have great versatility in the garden. Plant them to create blocks of color, make them a dramatic focal point in a garden design, or mix them with forget-me-nots and wallflowers, or with marguerites, for a soft, natural result. Use tall Fosteriana hybrids, which have the largest blooms, to produce a theatrical effect or gather double tulips in a massed bed to create a maximum impact of color. Dwarf and small species tulips will enhance the rock garden.

TULIPA 'GREENLAND' (LEFT) IS A
superb product of the
geneticist's art. Here is a
Viridiflora bloom that carries
a strong element of green, the
color normally reserved for
foliage, and in no slight hue
but as a pure, bright shade.
The stiff, closed cup of the
flower is designed to show
off the startling color
combination.

EMERGING PROUDLY FROM THEIR
loose, draped foliage, these
tulips (right), named
'Hummingbird', make a
bright cluster of color in the
garden. The petals take on the
shape of a graceful cup and
carry a delicate green stripe
up their center line.

'ARTIST' (LEFT) IS A VIRIDIFLORA
that deserves a special place
in the garden where its
strange beauty is neither
obscured nor obliterated by
any other plant. For those
who long for the original and
the beautiful, this is the tulip
that brings both qualities to
the garden.

In keeping with the trend toward maintaining and preserving wild plants, nurseries are now stocking an increasing range of species tulips. Although not strictly new in themselves, these tulips are being newly used in the garden in informal designs.

The species *Tulipa batalinii*, a native of Asia, is an excellent example of such an introduction. It is only 6 inches (15 cm) in height, but its perky, upright petals are a pretty sight in the spring garden. Even smaller, newly popular species such as *Tulipa tarda* grow to a mere 4 inches (10 cm) from ground level.

The Lily-flowered tulips, with open blooms and pointed, often reflexed, petals, have attracted the attention of breeders. They are available in a variety of sizes, to a maximum height of 28 inches (70 cm) and flower over a long period. These small tulips are ideally suited to growing in rock gardens.

THE SPECIES TULIPA BATALINII *(left) was once grown exclusively as a greenhouse subject, but modern breeding programs have produced a bloom of notable shape that can now be used outdoors in a sheltered place. 'White Triumphator' and 'Mariette' (above) are typical Lily-flowered tulips, bred for their petal shape and qualities of endurance. The frilled and furled bloom of 'Blue Parrot' (right) has a wide, loose formation, which gives the waxy texture of the petals a soft, melting appearance.*

'LILAC WONDER' (OVERLEAF) IS an outstanding dwarf variety that has been bred from wild tulips native to Iran.

SNOWFLAKES, TRILLIUMS, AND FRITILLARIES

As awareness for the world environment grows stronger, and with it a heightened appreciation of the fragility of plant life, so gardeners have become ever more eager to "rescue" wild flowers and grow them for posterity in the garden.

These three small, shy plants – the snowflake or *Leucojum*, *Trillium*, and the snake's head fritillary *Fritillaria meleagris* – are examples of such plants. None has been greatly developed by plant breeders but all have become newly popular with both nurserymen and gardeners, and it is worth looking out for the few new varieties bearing larger blooms in stronger or purer colors.

Growing conditions required by these three plants vary somewhat. Trilliums grow from rhizomes (swollen underground stems) and demand moist, well-drained soil in a shady position. Rhizomes should be set 3 to 4 inches (7.5 to 10 cm) deep, at any time from August to March.

Both snowflakes and fritillaries are produced from bulbs and will thrive in either sun or partial shade in well-drained soil. Snowflake bulbs should be planted 4 to 5 inches (10 to 12.5 cm) deep, snake's head fritillaries 4 inches (10 cm) deep.

GARDEN STYLE GUIDE

All three of these plants look best grown in clumps and bring a delicate air to the spring garden. Trilliums look most effective grown in drifts with hostas and erythroniums or planted in shady rock gardens or under trees. Put leucojums beneath deciduous trees or shrubs with snowdrops and crocuses as neighbors. The speckled coloration of *Fritallaria meleagris* is complemented by that of the wallflower, and its untidy, sometimes unsightly, stems can be effectively hidden by hostas; rodgersia will also serve this camouflaging purpose.

THE NEW-FOUND POPULARITY OF the snake's head fritillary (above) can be attributed to the extraordinary dappled quality of the bells.

THE NODDING BELLS OF THE snowflake (left) droop on wiry, slender stems. The newest varieties accentuate the delicate green tips on each of the petals.

THE TRILLIUM (RIGHT), IN A NEW deep purple shade, is sometimes grown on a raised bed where the shy blooms may be seen to best effect. In such a position, they still need leaf shade from above and leaves around them to help keep them cool and moist.

DAHLIAS

Although all dahlias are plants that propagate themselves vegetatively by means of underground tubers, they are generally divided by gardeners into border dahlias, which are grown from the tubers, and the smaller bedding dahlias, which are grown from seed and treated as tender annuals. All dahlias are also classified according to their flower shape. The most popular types include Single-flowered, Anemone, Collerette, Peony-flowered, Decorative, Pompon, Cactus, and Semi-Cactus.

Both border and bedding dahlias offer new developments in unusual flower formations, with petals that twist and curl, or spread in wide star shapes, or cluster in the tightest of pompons. Color, too, is wide and varied, and new hues and combinations, often in mottled or striped effects, are introduced each year.

Modern dahlias are easy to grow. Tubers of border dahlias can be started into growth in the greenhouse from mid-February. Cuttings taken when shoots are 3 inches (7.5 cm) high can be planted out in beds in medium to heavy soil, preferably in a sunny situation, once the risk of frost is past. Alternatively, the dry tubers can be planted directly into the border in late spring.

A JOYOUS DISPLAY IN THE garden, these 'Shandy' blooms (below) of a Cactus dahlia have the merit of a subtle color tone and fullness of flower.

'FLUTTERBY' (ABOVE), classified as a decorative type, tilts the ends of pointed petals and marks these with sharp color contrasts and delicate shading.

IN THE DAHLIAS GROUPED ON THE opposite page, 'Dana Audrey' (top left) is a decorative type bred in a new subtle color. A closely clustered heart opens generously at the base of the candy-striped Semi-Cactus 'Anatol' (top right). Delicate shaded and blended hues are the new feature in the Decorative 'Yelno Enchantment' (bottom left). An exciting new color combination of dark wine against sharp white is displayed by another Decorative dahlia 'Duet' (bottom right).

DAHLIAS

'Dandy' (above) is a dahlia distinguished by its unusual central frill of pale, quilled petals. This new variety of Collerette dahlia also comes in shades of yellow and orange. 'Harry Dunkley' (left) is a glorious golden ball of tightly packed petals and an exciting addition to the range of Pompon dahlias.

A superb result of creative breeding is displayed in 'Jura' (right). The unusual beauty of this Semi-Cactus dahlia will bring delight to any gardener.

GARDEN STYLE GUIDE

A late summer border can be one of vivid color, to which dahlias make a major contribution. The emphatic presence of the dahlia will give balance to plants with softer blooms such as cleomes. The taller varieties with large flowers can be grown in their own specimen bed, but the vivacity and variety of form in the dahlia give it an important role in border design. Plant dwarf varieties, particularly Pompons, in the rock garden.

IRISES

While the large irises of the herbaceous border grow from rhizomes, the smaller irises propagate themselves by means of bulbs. Among the prettiest of these is the petite *Iris reticulata*, a native of the Caucasus, which grows to a mere 6 inches (15 cm) in height and bears flowers up to 3 inches (7.5 cm) across in late February and early March. The plant gets its name from the netted or reticulate fibers that surround the bulb.

Many interesting hybrids have been developed in the flower form and color of these hardy plants, but these characteristically retain the yellow shading down the center of the petal. Latest hues include reddish purple and white.

Plant the bulbs 2 inches (5 cm) deep and 2 inches (5 cm) apart in well-drained soil containing plenty of organic matter. In severe winter weather protect plants with cloches.

'VIOLET BEAUTY' (OPPOSITE), while retaining a variation of the traditional blue, has been bred to bloom later in the season than the norm.

THE IRIS RETICULATA (BELOW left) is among the most interesting of the very small garden plants. It has a lovely fragrance, which has been retained by its hybrids. 'Natasha' (below) brings an entirely new feature in the form of its white bloom. Until recently, hybrids were confined exclusively to shades of blue – from a clear, pale hue to dark ultramarine.

GARDEN STYLE GUIDE

The flower of the reticulate iris is a line sketch of the grander, more flamboyant Bearded iris, yet it retains a dignified individuality. It is displayed to best effect in the rock garden, alone or with other miniature bulbs such as crocuses, narcissi, and snowdrops. These irises are also good border edging plants, where they mix well with spring-flowering daisies, anemones, and violas.

NARCISSI

The *Narcissus*, whose large-trumpeted form is called a daffodil, has a special place in the heart of gardeners, for traditionally this bloom is the herald of spring, the symbol of new growth and of warmth returning to the garden.

However, modern advances in genetic breeding and plant technology have altered the ancient spring rites of the narcissus. Breeders have worked to extend the natural flowering season, which means that it is now possible to obtain varieties that will bloom earlier than usual or later than expected. Narcissi can thus be used to bring their color into late winter garden, or their pleasure can be extended through until early summer.

The many varieties of narcissi are catalogued by the Royal Horticultural Society of Great Britain into 11 divisions, based on the length and shape of the trumpet or corona and the form of the petals.

As well as the many novel flower colors and forms now available, the species narcissi, most of them small in stature, have acquired a new-found popularity and use in the garden for both horticultural and ecological reasons. These species, totaling more than 60 in number, have been hunted by botanists and collectors for centuries and are increasingly being hybridized to extend their range of form.

GARDEN STYLE GUIDE

Narcissi are a charming sight when naturalized in drifts across the lawn or grouped under trees. They are also excellent for spring bedding designs; the species narcissi are ideal for rock gardens. Enhance their golden yellow tones by placing blue blooms among them.

The hoop petticoat, Narcissus romeuxii *(right) is a charming species narcissus. Nurseries are beginning to stock such species in response to new demands from gardeners to conserve such natural forms. Pendant flowers with long trumpet-shaped cups held by petals that curve and sweep back from the center typify the cyclamen-flowered narcissi such as 'Jack Snipe' (above). The more geometric lines of 'Hawera' (left), a triandrus type, show how the breeders can subtly alter the shape of the flower.*

NARCISSI

Although there are literally thousands of listed hybrids of narcissus, this has not deterred the breeders, who continue to experiment with new shapes, double blooms, and color mixes. Notable among the trends in new narcissi are double blooms in which the central trumpet is transformed into thickly fluffed and complex whorls; blooms with ruffled, split, central cups; the introduction of new colors, such as pink into the trumpet; and the breeding of flattened, disk-like flowers. In addition, the flower's natural yellows and golds have been strengthened, paled, and endlessly altered with subtle shading and tonal variation.

Narcissi should be planted in fall. All should be set at least 6 inches (15 cm) deep, with small bulbs set 2 to 3 inches (5 to 7.5 cm) apart, and larger ones 4 to 6 inches (10 to 15 cm) apart. Soil should be well drained. After flowering it is important that the leaves are not removed for six weeks, when they should have yellowed and died down.

IN THE LARGE-CUPPED NARCISSUS 'Passionale' (above) the trumpet has been bred to an unusual pink tone.

A GLORIOUS SPECIMEN OF artistic breeding, the unusual form of 'Petit Four' (right) is classed as a double narcissus.

THE SOFT BLOOM OF 'CASSATA' (left), a split-cupped narcissus, gives a gentle announcement to spring.

'CHANTERELLE' (RIGHT) IS A split-cupped variety with petals typically split for more than a third of their length. The bold orange tones are reminiscent of the wild mushroom whose name this narcissus shares.

'SUNDISC' (BELOW) HAS BEEN bred to exploit the simplicity of the "natural" shape of the narcissus. However, the trumpet of the bloom is so short that the flower is virtually flat – hence its name. Display this new variety in a prominent position where it will be the focus of attention.

THE DOUBLE 'TAHITI' (BELOW) reveals the breeders' art in both form and color mix.

LILIES

By nature, the lily is temperamental and demanding, satisfied only when given a great deal of attention. Because of this, many lilies remained, until recently, the domain of the true specialist.

The hybrid lily has abandoned this old volatile nature and has acquired a new vigor and ease of growth as well as blooms of increased size. It is also markedly less vulnerable to diseases such as basal rot than its predecessors. Judicious choice of new hybrids will provide lilies in flower from May through September.

Lilies are grown from bulbs which should be planted approximately 6 inches (25 cm) deep in well-drained soil, in sun or partial shade. Before planting, enrich the soil with plenty of compost, and water plants freely during the growing season.

'GRAND PARADISO' (RIGHT) HAS a waxed and modeled appearance, with a shiny color tone that suits this effect. Such a smooth monotone is not usual in the majority of lilies, which tend to be delicately marked and speckled, although the gleam and shine of color is a common trait.

THE LILY HAS AN ARCHITECTURAL form without the formality or ceremony that this implies. This attribute has been emphasized by many of the breeders: the hybrid 'Brushmarks' (right) has a softness of form and a delicate yellow shade dabbed into the center of each petal.

'JETFIRE' (OPPOSITE) IS A NEW hybrid with a crimson center contrasting with tangerine tips. A stippled effect in shades of deep pink and white has been perfected in the new hybrid 'Devon Dawn' (left), which is the result of a cross between Lilium auratum *and* Lilium speciosum.

LILIES

The lovely trumpet bloom of Lilium formosanum *'Priceii' is not diminished by the fact that it is borne on a miniature plant that grows to only about 12 inches (30 cm) – less than half the height of a lily such* *as a Madonna. Dwarf lilies such as these can be used in different ways from the traditional tall lilies, for example at the front of a border, as illustrated here, or in a rock garden.*

GARDEN STYLE GUIDE

The foliage of the lily has little impact once the finery of the flowers has faded. To ameliorate this effect, mix lilies with the floating blossom of *Astrantia major* or the pale clusters of *Helleborus orientalis*. Alternatively, mass lilies together in their own bed, in groups of similar size and/or color, or grow them in a tub.

GLADIOLAS AND TIGER FLOWERS

Both these splendid plants grow from corms and respond to similar treatment. The corms should be lifted and stored in winter, and planted out in spring in a place that will provide the sun, warmth, and moisture essential to vigorous growth.

For decades the gladiolus has been popular as a garden plant and an exhibition flower. There are hundreds of hybrids, bred to vary color and height and to improve the tender nature of the original genus. The shape of the blooms has also been altered, from plain trumpet-like forms to frilled flowers that look like butterflies. The new graceful miniatures are perfect for small town gardens.

Tigridia, the tiger flower, is native to Mexico. The few new hybrids have been developed so that these brilliant blooms may be grown by gardeners in both hemispheres. There has also been some experimenting with different colors, for the tigridia flower is a handsome and glossy blossom perfectly fashioned for breeding in a varied palette.

THE BREEDER'S PASSION FOR experimenting with the color of the gladiolus is revealed in this strange green trial bloom.

'ALBA' (LEFT) IS ONE OF THE RARE hybrids of Tigridia pavonia *(right), which is now cultivated by many nurseries; there is an increasing demand for this decorative plant, until now not widely available. It can be grown in a formal setting or allowed the freedom of a "wild" or naturalized garden look.*

124

SHRUBS

The breeding of new shrubs has succeeded in creating plants suited to smaller gardens and to urban ways of cultivation. Through their efforts, breeders have created plants that not only have flair and style beyond the simple utilitarian function of the garden shrub, but are also often usefully compact in habit.

Many shrubs have beautiful blossoms and this aspect has, of course, excited the breeders, but they have not confined their research to the flower forms. Gardeners appreciate the structure and texture of these leafy plants, and breeders have brought to the foliage subtle hues ranging from dusky blues, deep wine tones, and gray, to pure, clean greens, and variegated mixtures of all these. Sculptural leaf shapes or a rhythmic cascade of a leaf arrangement have also been introduced to previously demure foliage. A collection of shrubs should be able to supply decoration all year round, including winter color, without any special care.

The breeders have made great use of the natural tendency of many shrubs to "sport". Thus 'Sundance', the new yellow variety of choisya, arose from a "freak" yellow-leaved portion of an originally all-green plant. The natural species of many shrubs have also provided forms not previously cultivated. Often, as in *Syringa mayeri* 'Palibin', the miniature lilac, they have the advantage of small size.

❧

THE RHODODENDRON 'CYNTHIA' IS A GLORIOUS AND VIGOROUS recent variety that can grace a large garden. Many other new varieties of this shrub are greatly reduced in size and are suitable for growing in small gardens.

CAMELLIAS

There are many thousands of hybrids of the *Camellia*, not least because even amateur hybridists can have fun using pollen from different plants to create their own crosses. Of all the existing hybrids, *Camellia x williamsii* has been described as "one of the most valuable shrubs ever produced," and from it many of the best new hybrids have come. The other major source of new varieties is the common *Camellia japonica*.

It is not only the luscious bloom of waxy petals that makes the camellia a desirable ornament in the southern garden, it is also the plant's glossy, thick evergreen foliage. Breeders have concentrated on developing the flower color in all shades of red, pink, and white – and mixtures of all three – in all manner of single, semidouble, and double blooms.

The camellia has acquired an unfounded reputation for being difficult to cultivate. The only prerequisites for success are a good, lime-free, acid soil, which should be of a peaty consistency, and a warm climate. Given these, and preferably a sheltered position out of the wind and a cool root run, most are hardy plants needing little routine care.

The new camellia hybrids flower over a long period, and it is now possible to select a range that will provide blooms from October through to May. Flower sizes range from about 3 inches (7.5 cm) to a massive 7 inches (17.5 cm) across. Plants are available in upright or semiweeping forms, depending on variety, and many of the *C. x williamsii* hybrids are suitable for growing in pots. This method of cultivation is also ideal for gardeners whose soil is not naturally acid.

GARDEN STYLE GUIDE

In exposed areas, camellias will do best in the shelter of a wall or hedge. They can also be grown on a patio, provided they are not exposed to the sun before late afternoon. Most grow to about 10 feet (3 m), but there are new, shorter varieties now on the market. The deep, glossy foliage brings constant depth and color to an enclosed area and a pleasing accent to the formal garden. Ornamental cherries, for instance, which are leafless when in bloom, become sharply defined against the backdrop of the deep green foliage of the camellia.

CAMELLIA JAPONICA 'JUPITER' (top) is one of the best shrubs in the garden. The warm red flowers appear from February to May. 'Coppelia' (above) is a new carefree variety of C. x williamsii. *It does not even need deadheading, since the spent blooms will detach themselves from the plant. Like other camellias, these need no pruning except for the routine removal of any straggly, untidy shoots.*

THESE BEAUTIFUL PINK-EDGED blooms of Camellia sasanqua *'Rainbow' open from pure pink buds, reflecting the subtle effects that the breeders are now able to achieve. This frost hardy, densely foliaged camellia, which demands a sunny site in the garden, blooms in the fall. It will grow to about 10 feet (3 m) in height, with a maximum spread of some 5 feet (12 m).*

FUCHSIAS

The wild *Fuchsia* is a rare plant in its native lands of South America and New Zealand. However, the popularity of the cultivated fuchsia has led to extensive breeding, so that today there are at least 2,000 different hybrids. The forms of these fuchsias range from sprawling ground cover plants, through graceful "weeping" plant forms, to plants that have a very upright stature.

Botanically, the fuchsia is correctly categorized as a shrub, but in the garden the hybrids are more appropriate to the flower border, patio, or hanging basket than the traditional shrubbery. Some fuchsias are now even sold for use as mass bedding plants, reflecting the trend toward "instant gardening."

The charm of the fuchsia lies in the dangling flower, its petals turning in a dainty frill around an inner bell. Frost hardiness has been improved in many varieties, but those most commonly grown in the U.S. are cultivars of *F. hybrida*, which is not hardy; they are used as summer container plants.

GARDEN STYLE GUIDE

Fuchsias should be used in the garden in ways that make the most of their variations in habit. Upright types are best trained into standards or into compact bushes and as such can be successfully container grown. With the species it is even possible to create a fuchsia hedge. Those with a trailing or otherwise disciplined form can be trained on trellises or other supports, or grown in hanging baskets. The smallest types are suitable for growing in rock gardens. Less hardy types may prefer the shelter offered by a wall.

'PRESTON GUILD' (LEFT) IS A clear sugar pink but with subtle embellishments. The tube has deeper pink vertical stripes, and each sepal of the calyx is tipped with pale green. This is a semidouble bloom. In other new varieties, two shades of pink may define the separate parts of a semidouble flower. Like all fuschias, these will thrive in partial shade and well-drained soil.

THE SINGLE 'LEONORA' (ABOVE) is distinctive for its precise divisions of color. The tube and calyx are pure white, turning back from a violet corolla. Crimson stamens give this ensemble a designer note.

'Pink Marshmallow' (right), in complete contrast, is soft and crumpled in shape, and creamy in color. This double would make a marvelous cascade from a hanging basket.

LILACS AND MOCK ORANGES

The *Syringa*, or lilac, is a shrub popular for its gorgeously scented, densely clustered, tubular flowers. Breeders have worked on this over many years, to improve the size and fragrance of the blooms and to introduce new colors such as deep purples and pure whites. However, the large size of the traditional lilac – up to 20 feet (6m) – confined its presence to large gardens.

Now, the introduction of hybrid versions of dwarf species brings this lovely shrub within the compass of the small garden. These hybrids are often superior to the native ones in their decorative quality and hardiness. They can be grown anywhere except in really deep shade and in areas with long, hot summers.

The *Philadelphus*, or mock orange, is another hardy shrub grown for its scent. New varieties of this shrub are more bushy and compact than the older hybrids, which tend to be straggly in habit and of smaller dimensions. The best of the new hybrids include new double-flowered and golden- and variegated-leaved forms, and even plants that will withstand attack by industrial pollutants.

GARDEN STYLE GUIDE

Plant peonies or oriental poppies near a miniature syringa in a mixed bed, or place this shrub with Shrub roses and hardy geraniums. Whatever the choice of neighbors, think of the syringa in a color mix of pinks, creams, and mauves. A dwarf philadelphus with its dainty leaves and flowers is ideal for the back of the rock garden. Larger forms can be mixed with other shrubs in a garden design, as long as the blooms are well displayed.

THE SMALL PROPORTIONS OF Syringa meyeri 'Palibin', *planted in its own space, sit well against a stone walled background. The blooms are pale mauve and the foliage bright and fresh, but the plant does not have the rich scent of larger lilacs; the fragrance of the flowers and foliage is much more like that typical of a sweet privet.*

THESE TWO EXAMPLES OF philadelphus show how breeding can alter and improve flower forms. 'Enchantment' (right) is a perfect large fully double flower, while 'Manteau d'Hermine' (below right) carries a showy, semidouble bloom of creamy white. Both varieties have a wonderfully heady fragrance.

WEIGELAS, CHOISYAS, AND VIBURNUMS

These three shrubs are justifiable garden favorites that have been markedly improved by modern breeding. *Choisya* has been a favorite in warm climates for its neat, rounded form and shiny evergreen foliage. The newer hybrids have brought a lighter green or yellow hue to the leaf, but they retain the sweet scent that gives the plant its common name of Mexican orange blossom. It prefers a sheltered position in the garden with some sun.

Some viburnums, too, have a pleasing fragrance, but in these shrubs breeders have exploited the natural tiered branching of the *Viburnum plicatum tomentosum*. The result is a range of interesting forms in this versatile grow-anywhere shrub.

Until the advent of new hybrids, *Weigela* risked a fall in popularity because of its unwieldy growth form. Breeding has transformed this shrub into one of tidy, compact garden habits. Blooms of the new weigelas are pink, white, or yellow, and in one outstanding new variety red and cream blooms occur on the same plant. In other new hybrids, the leaves are yellow or variegated, or become tinged with purple as the summer progresses.

GARDEN STYLE GUIDE

Grow choisya next to the shrub *Ceanothus thrysiflorus* 'Cascade' and weigela adjacent to astrantia to create highly pleasing color combinations. Use the viburnum illustrated as a focal point, add it to an informal or wild garden design, or place it in a corner where its layered form will be best displayed.

THE FREE-FLOWERING AND dense blooms of Weigela *'Victoria' (left) are a charming addition to the garden now that breeding has confined the straggly growth of the native plant to neat proportions.*

GOLDEN LEAVES ARE THE NEW feature of Choisya ternata *'Sundance' (top right). This hardy shrub blossoms in May and will then bear star-shaped flowers sporadically throughout the summer.*

THE PLATE-SHAPED LACECAP blooms serve to emphasize the tiered branching of Viburnum plicatum tomentosum *'Shasta' (right).*

RHODODENDRONS

The genus *Rhododendron*, which also embraces the azaleas, contains at least 500 species, with hundreds of hybrid varieties. Rhododendrons are typified by thick, dark, evergreen or semievergreen leaves. Their foliage makes them valuable landscape plants, but the joy that they provide arises from the glory of their blooms. Indeed, the name derives from the Greek meaning "rose tree."

The soft loveliness of the rhododendron flower has inspired breeders to create additional levels of magnificence and caused botanists to search Asia for rare and undiscovered species. Some of the most recent and interesting developments in the breeding world have come from experiments on the species *Rhododendron yakushimanum*, a native of Japan. This is a dwarf species and the hybrids, sometimes known as Modern Compact rhododendrons, are only 24 inches (60 cm) high, with a spread of between 24 and 36 inches (60 and 90 cm).

This petite growth has appeal for many urban gardeners, and the geneticists have worked at developing a range of lovely hybrids. These are extremely hardy and bear flowers about 2 inches (5 cm) across during May and June; deadheading will help maximize the flowering period. Like all other rhododendrons, they demand a neutral to acid soil.

A large garden may provide the scope for magnificent groups of rhododendrons, but the dwarf varieties can be planted on a smaller scale, and even in tubs. Place them so that foliage and blossom offer their best by way of texture and display. To guarantee success, the site should be shady with perpetually moist soil.

'BASHFUL' (ABOVE) CARRIES clusters of double blooms quite different from those of R. yakushimanum 'Happy' (right), its close relation in the new Modern Compact series. Here the white flowers hold themselves loosely against dark purple foliage.

SHARP GREEN LEAVES characterize the R. yakushimanum 'Sleepy' (overleaf). The single blooms are numerous and are distributed in loose terminal clusters in great profusion all over the low and compact form of this shrub.

AZALEAS

The azalea is a member of the *Rhododendron* genus but differs from it in a variety of subtle ways. As a rule, the azalea is smaller, more fragile in its appearance, with more delicate foliage; botanically the azalea flower is distinguished by having only five stamens as opposed to the ten or more stamens of the true rhododendron.

Azalea hybrids abound. In those of the deciduous Knap Hill and Exbury hybrids, between 18 and 30 flowers may be gathered on a single stem. The other groups of azalea hybrids to which breeders have devoted particular attention are the Mollis azaleas and the evergreen Kurume hybrids, also known as Japanese azaleas. Among all the azaleas, new colors and color combinations, including bicolored stippled effects inside the flower, feature in the latest range of hybrids. Greater profusion of flowers, furling, and frilling of the petals and the creation of compact, dwarf forms, and extension of the flowering period are the other prominent trends in the apparently ceaseless breeding of new forms.

Most azaleas are hardy subjects as long as they are provided with an acid or neutral soil. In chalky or alkaline areas, the plants can be container grown. They prefer mild winters. Some will survive in sun, but most do best in dappled sunlight and prefer cool root runs. Placed in shade, the lovely hues assume a pale modesty which becomes "bleached" out in full sun. If plants become straggly, they may be lightly pruned to reshape them.

'Mrs Oliver Slocock' (left) is a Mollis hybrid of rich golds. The flowers appear before the leaves and so are shown off to perfection. 'Golden Sunset' (above) is an Exbury hybrid, typified by large trusses of flared blooms and attractive deciduous foliage.

GARDEN STYLE GUIDE

Such a blatantly profuse and gorgeous plant as the azalea demands its own special place. Grow two, three or more together and blend colors. Golds and yellows cause a shimmer; soft creams with bronzes, or pale pinks with purples make dreamy displays. Single bushes will create a focus in a small garden and azaleas can also be grown in ornamental tubs and urns to bedeck the summer patio.

THE ELEGANT SHAPE OF THE azalea with its profusion of blooms is demonstrated in 'Strawberry Ice' (above), a new Knap Hill hybrid of a high standard. After flowering, the foliage turns a flaming bronze to provide fall interest.

CLEMATIS

Clematis is a climber that grows wild in some temperate climates, and the various species generally carry small, bell-shaped flowers in pastel shades. In the nineteenth century an English botanist created a hybrid with large, star-shaped, flat flowers of an imperial purple. Its beauty inspired Victorian gardeners, and by the end of the century there were more than 300 hybrids, a few of which survive today.

Botanists are still experimenting with the clematis, and there are now some 200 hybrids. The new forms, most of which have vigorous habits, include a wide range of colors, both "pure" and with striped petal effects, and single and double blooms. Experiments are aimed at breeding clematis that will be even more hardy and, in particular, resistant to clematis wilt. Much work has also been done to introduce into garden cultivation new species discovered in diverse and exotic locations.

GARDEN STYLE GUIDE

A healthy hybrid clematis is a gorgeous sight in summer – a thick, tumbling vine starred with flat, open flowers. In some new hybrids, the bloom can measure 10 inches (25 cm) across. Train these strong climbers over walls, arbors, old stumps, or even over small trees.

'JOHN PAUL II' (ABOVE) HAS A clear, green foliage and very subtle pink stripes on the otherwise pure white petals, which open flat in a single bloom. This particular clematis looks very good against brick.

A CAREFULLY CREATED COLOR combination distinguishes 'Pink Champagne' (above). This climber should be placed in a prominent position where its dark beauty can be fully appreciated.

CRIMPED PETALS FLARE IN A double star shape in the true purple bloom of the new Japanese hybrid 'Hako Haken' (left).

CLEMATIS ALPINA 'WILLY' (right), with its half-open, pendant, bell-shaped flowers against bright foliage, is an outstanding new variant of a species clematis.

YUCCAS

The strange shape of the *Yucca*, stark and conspicuous, has made it attractive to gardeners who wish to add drama to their garden design.

Despite their exotic appearance, many yuccas do not demand a tropical climate or any extraordinary care, but have been developed to grow sturdily in the suburban garden. However, the plants do prefer a sunny site and well-drained soil.

Hybridization of yuccas has sought to vary the markings on the foliage, for instance, by developing stripes or margins of yellow that follow the green length of the swordlike leaves. The spectacular panicles of bell-shaped flowers also tempt breeders, so that both the height of the stem and the length of the panicles have undergone several changes. Some yuccas reveal very little stem and squat down in their spreading basal leaves; others grow taller than 72 inches (1.8 m).

Yuccas can be grown in large containers to decorate formal and patio gardens, where they should be kept well watered, especially when they are in a state of active growth.

GARDEN STYLE GUIDE

The yucca has a "presence" in the garden that calls for a space and an horizon of its own, especially if it is one of the taller of the breed. However, the shorter varieties are also grand enough to be given a spacious display. A yucca can take three years or more to bloom, but since it is evergreen, it will grace the garden with its stylish form even without the great, dangling blossoms.

'IVORY' IS A TALL, HANDSOME plant growing to 72 inches (1.8 m), with large panicles of bloom. Each flower of this modern variety is creamy white, very slightly tinged with green. This yucca will flower from mid- to late summer.

144

GARDEN DESIGNS

To inspire the use of new flowers in the garden, either alone or alongside the well-established favorites, eight original garden designs have been created for this book. They cover a range of sizes and situations, and most can be adapted for larger or smaller plots. Alternatively, specific features of individual designs can easily be incorporated into existing gardens.

The designs feature many new varieties additional to those illustrated in the previous pages, and are often chosen to fulfil specific needs in the individual garden plans, and to supply a wide variety of color and tone. It is important to take note of the aspect of each group of plants, since they have been carefully sited according to their needs for sun and shade.

This section is completed by a list of growers and seed suppliers from whom it should be possible to obtain the new flowers.

COUNTRY GARDEN

Where garden space is not at a premium, you can experiment widely with new plants. A larger country garden will be made more interesting if it is divided up into sections, especially if gaps are left between areas that allow only a glimpse of what lies beyond. Here, the area behind the rose garden is designed to encourage wildlife, especially butterflies and beneficial insects, into the garden.

There is plenty of room for shrubs, and year-round interest is provided by a section containing small winter heathers and dwarf shrubs. In winter, this will draw the eye away from the flowerless rose garden beyond. The large piece of ground near the house is the best place for a collection of the new varieties. Dahlias are suggested, but delphiniums, chrysanthemums, or any other plants with a long flowering period would be appropriate.

New flowers can be used in containers in the terrace area, to edge paths, and in more formal bedding designs.

1 *Berberis* 'Goldilocks'
2 *Philadelphus virginalis* 'Dwarf Snowflake'
3 *Spiraea trilobata* 'Swan Lake'
4 *Elaeagnus pungens* 'Gilt Edge'
5 *Pyracantha* 'Teton'
6 *Syringa* 'Sensation'
7 *Weigela* 'Rubygold'
8 *Buddleia davidii* 'Charming'
9 *Virburnum carlesii* 'Diana'
10 *Aster amellus* 'Nocturne'
11 *Rosa eglanteria* 'Sweet Briar'
12 *Mahonia aquifolium*
13 *Daphne* × *burkwoodii* 'Variegata'
14 *Viola* 'Molly Sanderson'
15 *Aurinia saxatilis* (*Allysum saxatile*) (3)
16 *Sedum spectabile* (3)
17 *Helenium* 'Red and Gold Hybrids'
18 *Aubretia* 'Cascade Strain'
19 Group of *Scabiosa* 'Blue Butterflies'
19a *Hemerocallis* 'Joan Senior'
20 *Armeria maritima* (3)
21 *Aster* × *frikartii* 'Mönch'
22 *Syringa meyeri* 'Palibin'

23 *Phlox maculata* 'Alpha' (3)
24 *Gaillardia* 'Double Mixed' (3)
25 *Solidago* 'Golden Thumb' (3)
26 *Wisteria sinensis*

Mini-arboretum containing:
27 *Acer palmatum* 'Ukigumo'
28 *Amelanchier arborea*
29 *Gleditsia triacanthos*
30 *Sorbus aucuparia*
31 *Betula pendula* 'Trost Dwarf'
32 *Prunus virginiana* 'Shubert'

33 Informal grass area containing primroses, snake's head fritillaries and foxgloves
34 "Flowering lawn" containing low-growing wildflowers
35 Large-flowered rose 'Silver Jubilee'
36 Patio rose 'Gentle Touch'
37 Miniature rose 'Snowball'
38 Modern Shrub rose 'Carefree Beauty'

39 *Salvia* 'Volcano' (summer) followed by *Hyacinthus* 'Blue Magic' to bloom in following spring
40 *Mimulus* 'Yellow Velvet' (summer) followed by *Narcissus* 'Baby Moon'
41 New dahlias (eg 'Anatol', 'Yelno Enchantment', 'Duet') followed by *Cheiranthus* 'Harlequin' and *Myosotis*, 'Blue Bouquet'
42 Ground cover roses (eg 'Red Bells', 'Cecile Brunner', 'The Fairy', 'Swany')
43 Large tubs containing *Lobelia* 'Blue Wings', *Impatiens* 'Cinderella' and *Dianthus* 'Princess Mixed' followed by ornamental kale
44 *Petunia* F$_1$ 'Giant Victorious' (summer) followed by *Primula* 'Pacific Giants' for winter
45 *Genista tinctoria* 'Golden Plate'
46 *Hebe* 'Margaret'
47 *Potentilla* 'Royal Flush'
48 *Euonymus* 'Sunspot'
49 *Skimmia* × *confusa* 'Kew Green'
50 *Erica carnea* 'John Kampa'

51 *Erica carnea* 'January Sun'
52 *Erica carnea* 'Vivellii'
53 *Erica darleyensis* 'Ghost Hills'
54, 55 *Erica vagans* 'Lyonesse'
56, 57 *Erica vagans* 'Cornish Cream'
58 *Erica darleyensis* 'J.W. Porter'
59 Bedding scheme of *Viola* F$_2$ 'Joker Mixed' followed by multibloom pelargoniums
60 *Clematis* 'Duchess of Edinburgh'
61 *Clematis* 'Pink Champagne'
62 *Clematis* 'Proteus'
63 *Clematis* 'John Paul II'
64 *Berberis thunbergii*
65 Hanging baskets of *Viola* F$_1$ 'Universal' in winter in warm climates or spring elsewhere, followed by tuberous *Begonia* 'Non Stop' in summer
66 *Abies koreana*

Garden measures approximately 130 feet (40m) by 120 feet (36m)

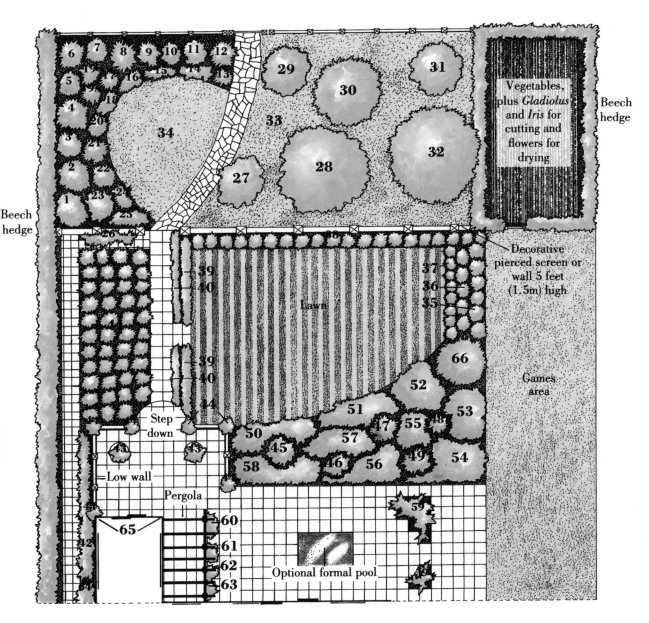

6 7 8 9 10 11 12
16 15 14 13
5 17 16
4 18
20 19
3 21
2 22
1 23 24 25
26 27

34

29
30
31
33
28
32
27

Vegetables,
plus *Gladiolus*
and *Iris* for
cutting and
flowers for
drying

Beech
hedge

Beech
hedge

Decorative
pierced screen or
wall 5 feet
(1.5m) high

Games
area

38
39
40
37
36
35

Lawn

39
40
44

66
52
51
53
50
17
55 48
45
57
50
58
46
56
49
54

Step
down

43
43

Low wall

Pergola

41
65
42
64

60
61
62
63

Optional formal pool

59

House

147

SMALL GARDEN

Color in this small garden is supplied by newer varieties of summer and spring bedding plants. A permanent framework – the other necessity in any garden, however small – is formed by the use of smaller species and varieties of shrubs, which are in increasing demand as garden space becomes ever more restricted.

The center circular bed is designed to take a garden ornament up to 36 inches (90 cm) high or a yucca – either a new form with variegated leaves or a large-flowered hybrid. This would complement the surrounding low-growing plants such as grasses. Lawn is impracticable in such a small area, and a much better effect is achieved using paving materials with different textures.

The low walls that surround the garden are not essential to the design. The mixed border to the front and west is intended to complement an open-plan frontage without walls or hedges. The plants included in this design will adapt to positions receiving more, or even slightly less, sunshine, but they must not be in total shade.

1 Miniature climbing rose 'Nozomi'
2 Hanging basket containing *Begonia* 'White Devil', *Lobelia* 'Blue Cascade', *Pelargonium* 'Scarlet Eye', *Calendula* 'Touch of Red' and variegated *Plectranthus*. If very shady use all *Impatiens* 'Starbright Mixed'. For winter use *Viola* F_1 'Universal Mixed'.
3 *Bergenia* 'Redstart'
4 Patio Rose 'Anna Ford'
5 Rose 'Snowball'

6 Garden ornament (36 inches/90 cm high) or *Yucca* 'Ivory'
7 Mixture of *Ophiopogon* 'Black Dragon', *Festuca ovina* var. *glauca* and *Acorus* 'Wogon'.
8 *Begonia* 'Non Stop' mixed
9 *Begonia* 'Pink Avalanche' (plant *Narcissus* 'Tahiti' or *Tulipa* 'Mariette' for spring)
10 *Dahlia* 'Rigoletto Mixed'

11 *Tagetes* 'Disco Orange' For spring bedding, use *Cheiranthus* 'Blood Red' (10) and *Bellis* 'Goliath' (11)
12 *Acer palmatum* 'Kagiri Nishiki' underplanted with:
13 Ground cover rose 'Rutland'
14 *Berberis* 'Telstar'
15 *Deutzia* × *rosea* 'Carminea'
16 *Althaea (Alcea)* 'Summer Carnival'
17 *Kniphofia* 'Maid of Orleans'

18 *Potentilla* 'Daydawn'
19 *Paeonia* – Japanese tree form
20 *Philadelphus* 'Manteau d'Hermine'
21 Primrose F_1 Hybrid 'Joker'
22 *Lavatera* 'Silver Cup', with *Narcissus* 'Sun Disc' naturalized beneath
23 *Digitalis* 'Temple Bells'
24 *Weigela* 'Victoria'
25 *Syringa meyeri* 'Palibin'

Garden measures approximately 16 feet (5 m) square

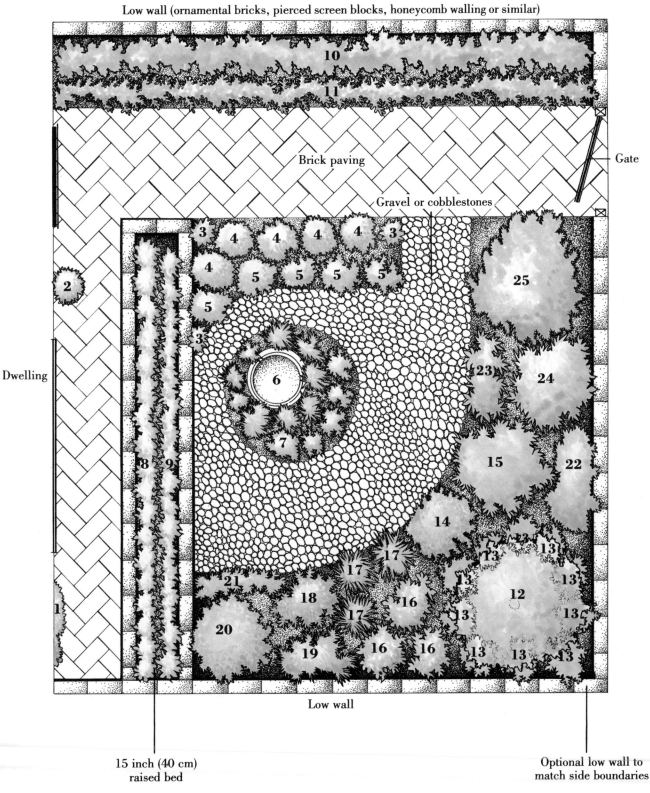

Low wall (ornamental bricks, pierced screen blocks, honeycomb walling or similar)

Brick paving

Gate

Gravel or cobblestones

Dwelling

Low wall

15 inch (40 cm)
raised bed

Optional low wall to
match side boundaries

COLOR THEME PATIO GARDEN

Silver, blue, gray, and green are the dominant colors in this theme garden. This color scheme is ideal for a hot, sunny area since it provides a cool restful feel. In fact, the plants chosen here demand the sunniest site possible. Without sun the gray- and silver-foliaged plants will neither last well nor produce their best color and form. Similarly, most of the plants with white or blue flowers prefer a sunny situation. The exceptions are blue-leaved hostas, which will tolerate full shade, and white *Begonia semperflorens* and busy lizzies.

It is not essential to incorporate a formal design into a color-theme garden, but it will work best if it is enclosed in some way. The effect is enhanced by the natural fragrance of the aromatic plants chosen, and by the use of highly fragrant summer jasmine and *Trachelospermum*. The scents will be most pronounced – and most appreciated – in an area that is warm and enclosed.

The scale of the design can be increased to fill a larger area by making the individual clumps of plants bigger and by widening the paving. Or it can be miniaturized by reducing the size of the central area and the surrounding beds.

1 Screen of *Chamaecyparis lawsoniana* 'Van Pelt'
2 Standard *Prunus* 'Shimidsu Sakura' underplanted with *Convallaria majalis*
3 *Pernettya mucronata* in warm climates, or *Juniperus chinensis* var. *sargentii* 'Glanca'
3a *Pernettya* (male form)
4 *Viburnum plicatum tomentosum* 'Shasta'
5 Statue or large urn containing *Campanula* F$_1$ 'Stella' in summer and variegated ivies in winter
6 *Cyclamen neapolitanum* var. *album*
7 *Arum italicum* 'Pictum'
8 Blue-flowered/glaucous-leaved shrub such as *Caryopteris clandonensis*
9 *Camellia* 'Cornish Snow'
10 Modern Shrub roses 'White Meidaland' (3)
11 *Tagetes* 'Sugar and Spice' underplanted with *Crocus* 'Bluebird'
12 *Hosta sieboldiana* 'Elegans'
13 *Chrysanthemum* 'Powder River'
14 *Anchusa capensis* 'Blue Angel' underplanted with *Scilla sibirica* 'Spring Beauty'

15 *Senecio maritima* 'Cirrhus'
16 Gray-leaved shrubs such as *Lavendula spica*
17 *Echinacea* 'White Swan'
18 *Ipomoea* 'Heavenly Blue'
19 *Philadelphus* 'Manteau d'Hermine'
20 *Viola* F$_1$, 'Universal White'
21 Climbing rose such as 'White Cockade'
22 *Delphinium* 'Can Can', 'Casa Blanca,' and 'Bellamosa' grouped
23 *Campanula pyramidalis* 'Blue and White Mixed'
24 *Ceanothus* 'Frosty Blue' in warm climates or *Viburnum carlesii* elsewhere
25 *Sambucus nigra pulverulenta*
26 White fragrant climber such as *Trachelospermum jasminoides*
27 Group of *Lilium formosanum* 'Priceii'

28 Gray-leaved dwarf shrub such as *Santolina chamaecyparissus*
29 Glaucous-leaved dwarf shrub such as *Ruta* 'Jackman's Blue'
30 *Clematis* 'Duchess of Edinburgh'
31 *Wisteria floribunda* 'Alba'
32 *Clematis* 'John Paul II'
33 White fragrant climber such as *Jasminum officinale*
34 Group of *Lilium* F$_1$ hybrids 'Everest'
35 Gray-leaved dwarf shrub such as *Santolina chamaecyparissus*
36 Gray-leaved dwarf perennial such as *Artemisia* 'Silver Mound'
37 *Weigela* 'Bristol Snowflake'
38 *Clethra alnifolia*
39 *Potentilla fruticosa* 'Abbotswood Silver'
40 *Lathyrus* 'Jilly'
41 Gray-leaved blue-flowered plant (eg *Perovskia atriplicifolia* 'Blue Spire')
42 *Deutzia gracilis*
43 *Clematis* 'Mrs George Jackson'
44 *Delphinium grandiflorum* 'Blue Mirror'

45 *Dianthus allwoodii* 'Arthur' underplanted with white *Crocus*
46 *Ageratum* 'Blue Danube'
47 Purple and white *Iris reticulata* overplanted in late spring with *Lobularia maritima* 'Snow Crystals'
48 *Deutzia gracilis* 'Nikko'
49 White-flowered early wall shrub (eg *Chaenomeles nivalis*)
50 Silver/green variegated shrub, (eg *Euonymus* 'Emerald Gaiety')
51 *Euphorbia marginata* 'White Top'
52 *Begonia* 'Olympia White'
53 *Chrysanthemum frutescens* (marguerite) with *Viola* 'Joker' (white) in centre of bed and *Matricaria recutita* around edge. (Bed planted with *Tulipa* 'White Triumphator' in spring.)

Garden measures approximately 20 feet (6m) by 30 feet (9m)

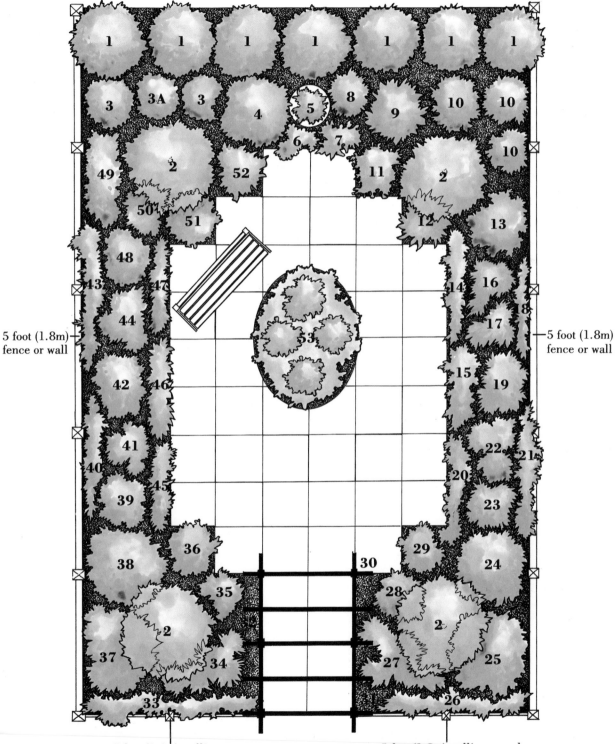

5 foot (1.8m)
fence or wall

5 foot (1.8m)
fence or wall

5 foot (1.8m) trellis
covered with *Jasminum officinale*

5 foot (1.8m) trellis covered
with *Trachelospermum jasminoides*

FRONT GARDEN

A garden in front of the house can pose design problems, especially if cars and other vehicles have to be accommodated within the area. This garden has been planned to create some privacy, while allowing visibility for drivers entering the road plus adequate parking and turning space.

A border of well-shaped shrubs and interesting bedding plants shields the house from the road and softens the effect of the turning bay. The shrubs must not be capable of growing too large, or they will create an unwanted enclosed effect. A feeling of height can be created, if desired, by the inclusion of one or two trees.

The clean lines of the design are echoed in the formal bedding design. The small bed of roses on the right-hand side of the driveway could be replaced with heathers and conifers, or with a collection of dwarf shrubs, if preferred.

1 Hanging baskets of *Impatiens* 'Accent' series (summer only)
2 Patio rose 'Rosabell' or rose 'Pink Pollyanna'
3 *Caragana pygmaea*
4 Standard Shrub rose 'Ballerina' underplanted with *Lobelia erinus* 'Rosamund'
5 *Betula pendula* 'Trost Dwarf'
6 *Bergenia* 'Evening Glow'
7 *Berberis thunbergii* 'Crimson Pygmy'
8 *Tulipa* 'Lilac Wonder' preceded in warm climates by *Viola* 'Baby Franjo'
9 *Narcissus* 'Jack Snipe' followed by *Nicotiana* 'Nicki Mixed'
10 *Muscari comosum* followed by *Impatiens* 'Blue Pearl'
11 *Viburnum dilatatum* 'Catskill'

12 *Philadelphus* 'Minnesota Snowflake'
13 *Weigela florida* 'Minuet'
14 *Chrysanthemum* 'Naomi'
15 *Chrysanthemum* 'Donna'
16 *Chrysanthemum* 'Nicole'
17 *Hypericum androsaemum*
18 *Viola* 'Jolly Joker' or *Primula* 'Rosebud Mixed'
19 *Skimmia japonica* 'Nymans'
20 *Cytisus* 'Dukaat'
21 *Hydrangea macrophylla* 'Pink 'n Pretty'
22 *Skimmia japonica* 'Wisley'
23 *Spiraea japonica* 'Golden Princess'

24 *Begonia × semperflorens cultorum* 'Brandy'
25 *Potentilla fruticosa* 'Sunset'
26 *Choisya ternata* 'Sundance'
27 *Viburnum plicatum* var. *tomentosum* 'Shasta'
28 *Deutzia gracilis* 'Nikko'
29 *Skimmia reevesiana*
30 *Hebe* 'Margret'
31 *Hyacinthus* 'Blue Magic' followed by *Dianthus* 'Black and White Minstrels'
32 *Juniperus squamata* 'Holger'
33 *Euonymus* 'Golden Prince'
34 *Juniperus horizontalis* 'Banff'
35 *Euonymus* 'Golden Prince'

36 *Juniperus horizontalis plumosa* 'Youngstown'
37 *Euonymus fortunei* 'Canadale Gold'
38 *Lavatera* 'Mont Blanc'
39 Standard *Fuchsia* 'Preston Guild', 'Leonora' and 'Pink Marshmallow'
40 *Begonia* 'Frilly Red' followed by *Myosotis* 'Carmine King'
41 *Crocus* 'Eyecatcher' followed by *Convolvulus* 'Blue Ensign'
42 *Pyracantha* 'Teton'

Garden measures approximately 32 feet (10m) by 50 feet (15m)

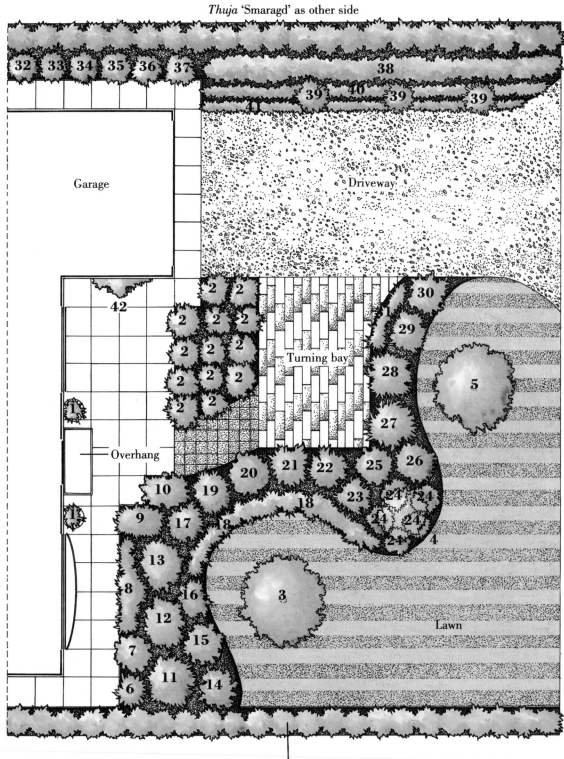

Thuja 'Smaragd' as other side

Garage

Driveway

House

Overhang

Turning bay

Lawn

Optional hedge of *Thuja* 'Smaragd' (or ornamental walling or range fencing)

LONG, NARROW GARDEN

Long, narrow gardens present the designer with a variety of problems. However, dividing the garden into sections, as has been done here, will create a better proportioned effect. This plan consists of a patio area adjacent to the property, a central paved area, and a third, enclosed area. The last of these is almost concealed by trellis fencing that supports two types of new ground cover roses, in this instance trained as well-behaved miniature climbers. The arch supports a new variety of clematis, and the eye is tempted to explore beyond this by a "path" of different types of paved surfaces crossing the center part of the garden.

Walls and fences throughout this design are used to advantage as support for climbing plants. The new flowers chosen for the beds create a balance between cheerful, temporary bedding plants and a nucleus of permanent herbaceous plants and shrubs, plus one or two small trees.

If the garden is squarer in shape, one or more of these sections can be omitted without spoiling the overall effect of the scheme.

1 *Tagetes* 'Discovery'
2 *Petunia* 'Red Stripe' (*Crocus sieberi* 'Pink Giant' in early spring)
3 *Jasminum officinale* 'Argentea Variegatum'
4 Pedestal vases containing *Pelargonium* 'Apple Blossom' (hyacinths in spring)
5 *Narcissus* 'February Silver'
6 *Lilium* 'Artist'
7 Charm *Chrysanthemum* 'Bull Finch'*
8 Charm *Chrysanthemum* 'Ring Dore'*
9 Charm *Chrysanthemum* 'Morning Star' *
10 *Papaver* Windsong 'Summer Breeze' (*Crocus* 'Sir Matthew Wilson' in winter)
11 *Zinnia* 'Miniature Pom-Pom' (*Crocus* 'Grand Yellow' in early spring)

12 Charm *Chrysanthemum* 'Ogmore Vale'*
13 Charm *Chrysanthemum* 'Tang'*
   * In colder areas use Margaret *Chrysanthemum*. Lift and store over winter in cold, light place and plant area in fall with new varieties of tulips.
14 *Hypericum androsaemum* 'Variegata'
15 *Spiraea japonica* 'Golden Princess'
16 Rose 'Drummer Boy'
17 *Hydrangea quercifolia*
18 *Lavatera* 'Mont Blanc' (new varieties of *Narcissus* in early spring)
19 *Buddleia davidii* 'Nanho Purple'
20 *Fuchsia fulgens gesneriana*

21 Ground cover rose 'Grouse' trained as a miniature climber
22 Ground cover rose 'Partridge' trained as a miniature climber
23 *Hebe* 'Blue Clouds'
24 *Clematis* 'Hako Hakan' or other Japanese variety
25 *Clematis alpina* 'Willy'
26 Ground cover rose 'Red Max Graf' trained as climber
27 *Berberis* 'Telstar'
28, 29 *Actinidia chinensis kolomikta* (28 & 29 edged with *Nemesia strumosa* 'Tapestry')
30 *Clematis montana* 'Tetrarose' (pink tetraploid) rambling over summerhouse or greenhouse
31 *Acer palmatuan* 'Burgundy Lace'
32 *Pyracantha* 'Teton'
33 *Polystichum aculeatum* (3)

34 *Paeonia lactiflora* 'Cherry'
35 *Papaver* 'Curlilocks'
36 *Crocosmia* 'Solfatare' or 'Lucifer'
37 *Aquilegia* McKana's hybrid
38 *Digitalis* 'Temple Bells'
39 *Wisteria* 'Royal Purple'
40 *Viola* 'Princess Blue'
41 *Hosta* 'August Moon' (3)
42 *Hebe* 'Margaret'
43 *Mallus* 'Red Jade' (crab apple)
43a *Thuja plicata* 'Irish Gold'
44 *Abutilon* 'Albus' (grow in pot and bring indoors for winter in all but the warmest climates)
45 Tuberous *Begonia* 'Nonstop'
46 Hanging basket of *Impatiens sultanii* F_1 'Super Elfin' (*Viola* F_1 'Universal' for winter)

Garden measures approximately 52 feet (15m) by 20 feet (6m)

Garden surrounded by fences or walls

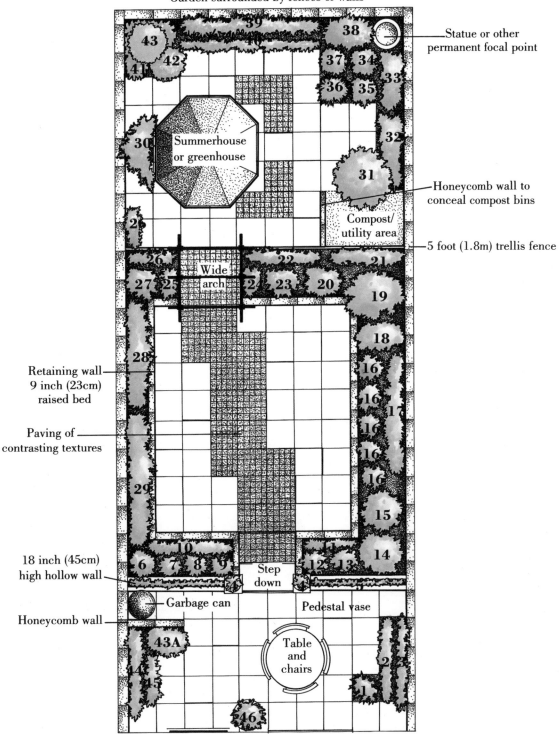

Statue or other permanent focal point

Honeycomb wall to conceal compost bins

5 foot (1.8m) trellis fence

Summerhouse or greenhouse

Compost/ utility area

Wide arch

Retaining wall 9 inch (23cm) raised bed

Paving of contrasting textures

18 inch (45cm) high hollow wall

Garbage can

Honeycomb wall

Pedestal vase

Step down

Table and chairs

Dwelling

WILDLIFE GARDEN

Even the smallest piece of land can contribute toward wildlife conservation. This garden is designed to incorporate a wide variety of natural features. In a smaller garden, even one or two of them will significantly increase the number of creatures visiting or making a home in your plot.

Seed houses and nurseries are responding to this new trend in gardening by supplying seeds and plants suitable for creating a wildlife garden. On no account should you attempt to obtain your stocks by decimating the countryside. Here, berrying trees provide food for birds, and the branch framework establishes nesting sites; their flowers encourage insect visitors. The mixed hedge of flowering and fruiting species achieves the same objective. Wild flowers can be introduced in a number of ways: on their own, mixed with grasses, with garden flowers in mixed border plantings, or in a "flowering lawn." The pond will attract aquatic creatures such as frogs, toads, and newts.

A garden that is ecologically sound should not be messy, but need not be obsessively tidy. Possums and other small animals will want places in which to shelter and to hibernate.

Area A
A bank 36 inches (90 cm) high planted with bluebells, species daffodils, forget-me-nots, celandines, winter aconites, primroses, and dog-tooth violets in a low maintenance mix of grasses.

Areas B and J
Mown patch of low-growing wild flowers.

Areas C and D
Informal shrubbery of:
1 *Viburnum opulus*
2 *Salix caprea*
3 *Hippophae rhamnoides*
4 *Ulex europaeus*
5 *Berberis koreana*
6 *Viburnum lantana*
7 *Hypericum androsaemum*
8 *Corylus avellana*
9 *Berberis thunbergii*
10 *Symphoricarpus*
11 *Cornus sericea*
Ground around these shrubs sown with wild white clover.
12 *Sorbus americana*
13 *Malus huphensis*
14 Arch of *Lonicera*

Area E
Ground planted with wood-edge wildflowers (eg foamflowers, phlox, etc.)

Area F
A mixed flower border to attract butterflies, bees and birds comprising:
15 *Solidago* 'Cloth of Gold'
16 *Antirrhinum* 'Magic Carpet Mixed'
17 *Nicotiana* 'Domino White'
18 *Rudbeckia* 'Goldsturm'
19 *Helianthus* 'Chrysanthemum Flowered'
20 *Gaillardia* 'Double Mixed'
21 *Lobularia maritima* 'Carpet of Snow'
22 *Reseda odorata*
23 *Centranthus ruber*
24 *Sedum spectabile*
25 *Monada* 'Croftway Pink'
26 *Achillea* 'Great Expectations'
27 *Aster* Dwarf Comet 'Pastel Blue'
28 *Eryngium giganteum*
29 *Chrysanthemum maximum* 'Polaris'
30 *Aster* × *frikartii*
31 *Scabiosa caucasica*
32 *Iberis* 'Dwarf Fairyland Mixed'
33 *Layia platyglossa*
34 *Cosmos* 'Sea Shells'
35 *Coreopsis grandiflora*
36 *Oenothera biennis*
37 *Nepeta mussinii*
38 *Tagetes* 'Disco Orange'

Area G
A wetland area formed by allowing a pond to run over into an area of soil placed over polythene to restrict drainage and planted with wild flowers:
39, 49, 56 *Chelone* sp.
40 *Lobelia cardinalis*
41, 48, 57 *Saururus cernuus*
42, 46 *Lythrum salicaria*
43 *Acorus calamus*
44 *Pontaderia cordata*
45 *Filipendula* sp.
47, 50 *Silene dioica*
51, 60 *Ranunculus acris*
52 *Iris pseudacoris*
53 *Achillea ptarmica*
54 *Impatiens capensis*
55, 59 *Eleocharis montevidensis*
58 *Ranunculus ficaria*
61 *Cardamine pratensis*
61A *Althaea officinalis*

Area G1
Shallow water provided by shelf in pond containing:
62 *Mentha aquatica*
63 *Sagittaria sagittifolia*
64 *Caltha palustris* 'Alba'
65 *Pontaderia cordata*
66 *Caltha palustris*
67 *Canna* 'Longwood Hybrids'

Area H
A collection of wild flowers attractive to wildlife arranged as a small border including:
68 *Hypericum prolificum*
69 *Chrysanthemum leucanthemum*
70 *Dipsacus fullonum*
71 *Stachys officinalis*
72 *Centaurea* sp.
73 *Armeria maritima*
74 *Echium* sp.
74A *Primula veris*

Area I
Rockery type planting of small species attractive to bees, butterflies and other beneficial insects eg:
75 *Armeria juniperifolia*
76 *Aurina saxatilis* 'Compactum'
77 *Phlox douglasii* 'Red Admiral'
78 *Solidago virgaurea*
79 *Aubretia* 'Purple Cascade'
80 *Helianthemum* 'Ben Nevis'
81 *Arabis alpina*

Garden measures approximately 60 feet (18m) by 40 feet (12m)

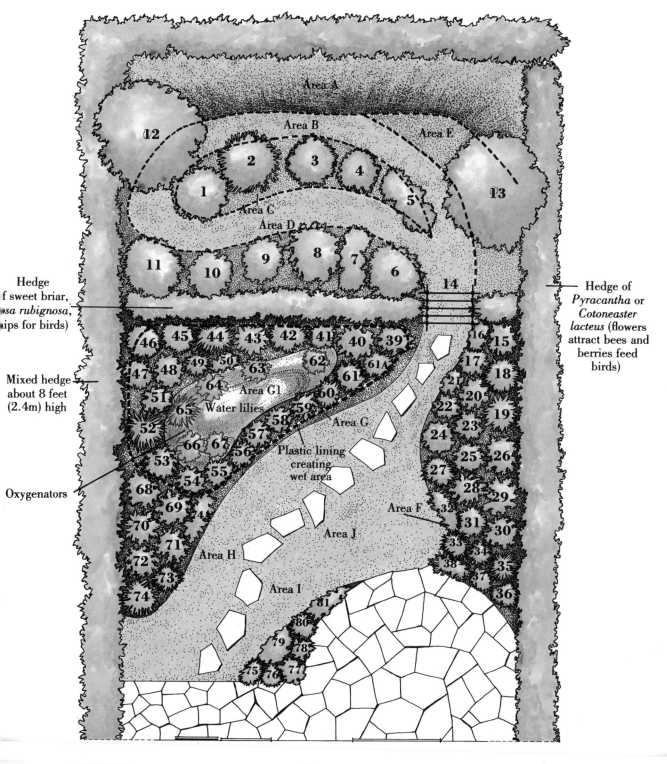

Area A

Area B

Area E

12

2

3

4

Area C

1

5

13

Area D

11

10

9

8

7

6

14

Hedge
of sweet briar,
Rosa rubignosa,
hips for birds)

46 45 44 43 42 41 40 39

16 15

47 48 49 50 63 62 61A 61

17 18

21 20

Mixed hedge
about 8 feet
(2.4m) high

51 64 Area G1 60 22 23 19

65 Water lilies 59 Area G 24 25 26

52 58 57 27

66 67 56 Plastic lining
creating
wet area

53 55

68 54 Area F 32 28 29

69 4 31 30

70 Area J 33 34

71 38 35

72 Area H 37

73 Area I

74 81 80 36

Oxygenators

79 78

75 76 77

Hedge of
Pyracantha or
*Cotoneaster
lacteus* (flowers
attract bees and
berries feed
birds)

House

157

ALL-YEAR-COLOR GARDEN

New flowers have been used in this garden to create color and interest all the year through. There is no difficulty in making a garden colorful during the summer months, using bedding plants, summer-flowering shrubs, and herbaceous perennials. More difficult, however, is to sustain this effect.

Evergreens, especially those newcomers with variegated leaves, can brighten up a winter garden. Ideally they should be mixed with a range of shrubs that will flower in late fall, winter and early spring fo an ever-changing garden aspect. Shrubs can contribute year-round interest in other ways, for example by producing catkins, or bright fruits or berries that remain on the plant well into winter. The dividing hedge of *Pyracantha* 'Teton', which is upright and free-flowering with profuse winter berries, has been chosen here for this purpose.

To enliven massed plantings of roses or herbaceous perennials, which are uninteresting after they have flowered and been cut back, plant up the space around them with early-flowering bulbs of shorter habit. Any untidy leaves of these plants that remain after flowering will quickly be camouflaged by the rapid spring growth of the shrubs.

1 *Malus* 'Red Jade' trees
2 Dividing hedge of *Pyracantha* 'Teton'
3–6 *Rhododendron yakushimanum* hybrids, 'Sleepy', 'Bashful' and 'Happy'
7 *Erica carnea* 'January Sun'
8 *Erica carnea* 'John Kampa'
9 *Erica carnea* 'Heathwood'
10 *Erica cinerea*
11 *Erica carnea* 'Westwood Yellow'
7–11 Heathers underplanted with *Tigridia pavonia*
12 *Cotoneaster hybridus pendulus* or 'Dammerii' trained as a standard
13 Raised bed containing *Primula* 'Rosebud Hybrids' in winter in warm climates and *Verbena* 'Showtime' in summer

14 *Actinidia kolomikta*
15 *Actinidia kolomikta* (plant *Hyacinthus* 'Blue Magic' at base for spring display)
16 *Syringa meyeri* 'Palibin'
17 *Spiraea trilobata* 'Swan Lake'
18 *Skimmia japonica*
19 *Celosia* 'Pink Castle' followed by *Gazania* 'Silverleaf Carnival'
20 Ornamental kale 'Nagoya Hybrid White on Green' (in warm climates followed with *Pelargonium* 'Lavender')
21 *Forsythia viridissima* 'Bronxencis'
22 *Ilex × meserveae* 'Blue Boy'
23 *Weigela* 'Victoria'
24 *Salix helvetica*
25 *Skimmia reevesiana*
26 *Viburnum × burkwoodii* 'Mohawk'
27 *Syringa meyeri* 'Palibin'
28 *Cytisus* 'Lena'
29 *Cornus mas* 'Aurea'
30 *Althaea (Alcea)* 'Summer Carnival'

31 *Tulipa* 'Hummingbird' followed by *Salpiglossis* 'Casino Mixed'
32 *Muscari comosum* followed by *Lobuleria maritimia* 'Sweet White'
33 Modern English Shrub rose 'English Garden'
34 Modern English Shrub rose 'Mary Rose'
35 Modern English Shrub rose 'William Shakespeare'
36 Modern English Shrub rose 'Heritage' 33–36 underplanted with *Narcissus* 'Chacha', 'Chanterelle' and 'Hawera' (back) and miniature *Narcissus bulbocodium* (front)
37 *Wisteria floribunda* underplanted with *Trillium grandiflorum*
38 *Clematis languinosa* 'Candida' underplanted with *Leucojum*
39 *Dahlia* 'My Love', 'Cheerio', and 'Harry Dunkley' (for spring plant *Tulipa batalinii* 'Greenland')

40 *Viburnum* 'Chesapeake'
41 *Cornus alba* 'Sibirica Variegata'
42 Climbing rose 'New Dawn'
43 *Gazania* 'Olympia Mixed' underplanted with green *Gladiolus*
44 *Antirrhinum* 'Little Darling'
45 *Chaenomeles speciosa*
46 *Hypericum prolificum* 'Hidcote'
47 *Pansy* 'Floral Dance Mixed' followed by *Begonia* 'Party Fun'
48 Urn containing *Viola* 'Universal F_1' followed by *Fuchsia* 'Pink Marshmallow'
49 *Elaeagnus pungens* 'Gold Rim'
50 *Ribes sanquineum* 'Tydeman's White'
51 *Spiraea japonica* 'Goldflame'
52 *Ampelopsis brevipeduculata* 'Elegans' underplanted with *Galanthus nivalis*
53 *Hydrangea quercifolia*

Garden measures approximately 60 feet (18m) by 35 feet (10m)

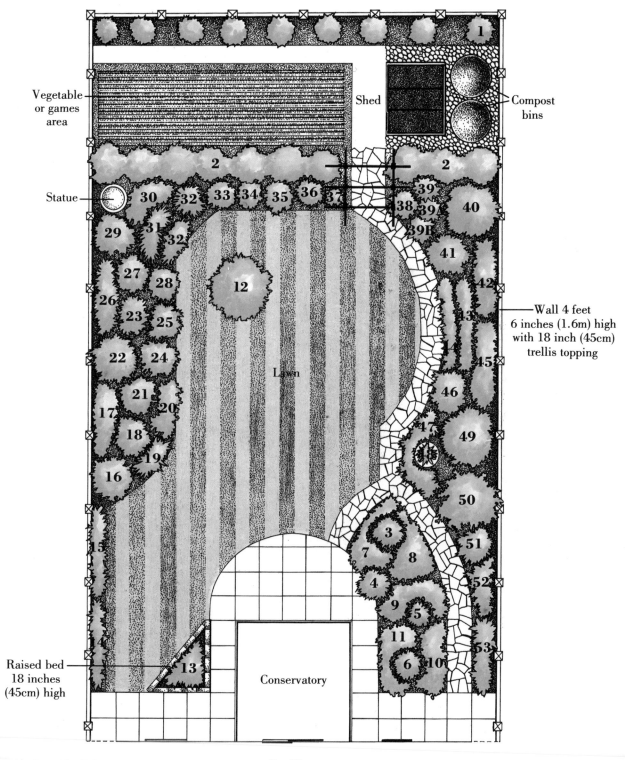

Vegetable
or games
area

Shed

Compost
bins

1

2

2

Statue

30

32

33 34

35

36 37

39

38 39

40

29

31

32

39F

27

28

26

23

25

12

41

42

22

24

43

Wall 4 feet
6 inches (1.6m) high
with 18 inch (45cm)
trellis topping

44

45

21

20

46

17

18

47

19

48

49

16

50

15

3

51

7

8

4

52

9

5

14

11

13

6

10

53

Raised bed
18 inches
(45cm) high

Lawn

Conservatory

Dwelling

159

FORMAL WATER GARDEN

The formal pool, incorporated into a modern garden setting, is the focal point of this design in which new flowers are used to help create an overall effect that is cool and restful. Aquatic plants have been used in moderation so that they do not overrun the pool and detract from its charm.

In the garden surrounding the pool, large shrubs have been omitted, since they will eventually become too bushy and spoil the garden's formality. Instead, climbing plants and those capable of being wall trained have been substituted, and the garden is provided with a permanent structure by the use of modern, more compact shrubs.

This garden has a "cool" side (the one in most shade), with a restful planting of ferns and other, mainly foliage, perennials. The area receiving more sunshine is given a brighter atmosphere through the use of bedding plants and bulbs, coordinated in shades of white, blue, lilac, and pink that do not detract from the tranquil feeling the water endows.

1 *Iris sibirica* 'Flight of Butterflies'
2 *Osmunda regalis*
3 *Hosta* 'Krossa Regal'
4 *Camellia* 'Taylor's Perfection' (grow in container in cooler climate)
5 *Dianthus chinensis* 'Pink Flash'
6 *Fragaria* 'Pink Panda' (3)
7 *Begonia* 'Olympia White'
8 *Pieris japonica* 'White Cascade'
9 *Lobelia* 'Kaleidoscope' or *Bellis* 'Clutch of Pearls'
10 *Clarkia elegans* 'Royal Bouquet'
11 *Parthenocissus tricuspidata* 'Robusta'
12 *Senecio* 'Silver Dust'
13 *Ageratum* 'Pink Powderpuffs' or *Myosotis* 'Carmine King'
14 *Hibiscus moscheutos* 'Discobelle White'

15 *Betula pendula* 'Frost's Dwarf'
16 *Viola* 'Universal White' followed by *Dahlia* 'My Love'
17 *Iris* 'Raspberry Blush'
18 *Virburnum* × *burkwoodii* 'Mohawk' trained against wall
19 *Impatiens* 'Lilac Pearl'
20 *Delphinium* 'Clifford Lass' or 'Blue Springs'
21 *Lobularia maritima* 'Snow Crystals'
22 *Escallonia* 'Red Elf'
23 *Magnolia stellata* 'June'
24 *Anagallis*, blue hybrid
25 *Dianthus* 'Telstar Picotee'
26 *Sambucus canadensis*

27 *Philadelphus* 'Manteau d'Hermine' or 'Dwarf Snowflake'
28 *Juniperus scopulorum* 'Blue Heaven'
29 *Heuchera* 'Palace Purple' (3)
30 *Crocosmia* 'Jenny Bloom'
31 *Filipendula ulmaria* 'Aurea'
32 *Dicentra spectabilis* 'Alba'
33 *Weigela* 'Victoria' or 'Bristol Snowflake'
34 *Pelargonium* 'Apple Blossom'
35 *Clematis* 'Niobe'
36 *Helleborus orientalis*
37 *Hemerocallis* 'Catherine Woodbury'
38 *Dryopteris erythrosora*
39 *Lonicera periclymenum* 'Graham Thomas'
40 *Astilbe arendsii* 'Rheinland'

41 *Houttuynia cordata* 'Chameleon'
42 *Hosta* 'Fringe Benefit' or 'Great Expectations'
43 *Matteuccia struthiopteris*
44–46 *Chrysanthemum indicum* 'Autumn Glory' – mixed colors – one plant per container, followed in spring by *Tulipa* 'Mariette', 'White Triumphator' and 'Hummingbird'
47 Standard *Salix helvetica* or other standard compact *Salix* in tub
48 *Caltha palustris* 'Alba'
49 *Pontaderia cordata*
50 *Nymphaea* 'Fire Crest'
51 *Nymphaea* 'Virginalis'
52 *Typha minima*
53 *Menyanthes guttatus*

Garden measures approximately 30 feet (9m) by 16 feet (5m)

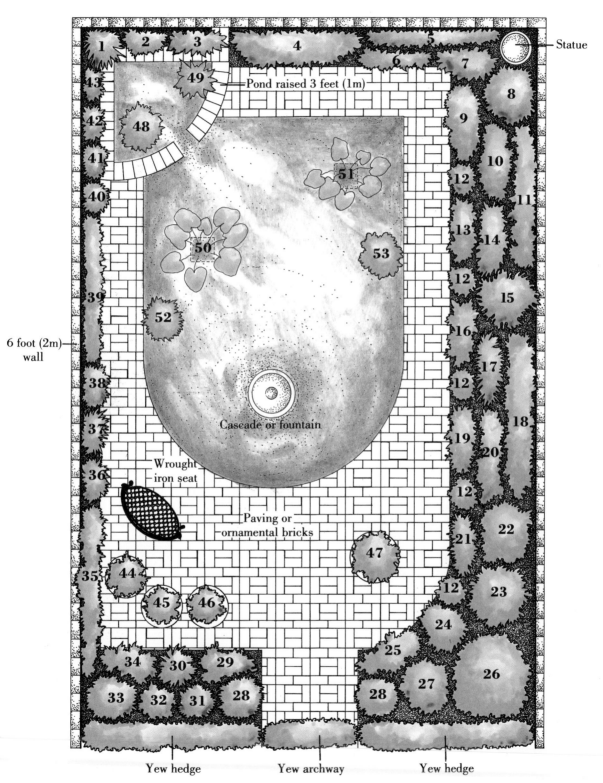

Statue

Pond raised 3 feet (1m)

Cascade or fountain

6 foot (2m) wall

Wrought iron seat

Paving or ornamental bricks

Yew hedge   Yew archway   Yew hedge

NURSERIES AND SUPPLIERS

The following companies supply catalogs. Many also operate a mail order system by which plants can be obtained. It is worth visiting your local supplier, where you may be able to make specific requests or place orders.

Bluestone Perennials
7211 Middle Ridge Rd.
Madison, OH 44057
Good selection of perennials

W. Atlee Burpee Co.
Warminster, PA 18974
Seeds of vegetables, herbs, and annuals; perennial seeds and plants; shrubs, vines, and other ornamentals; bulbs

Busse Gardens
Rte. 2, Box 238
Cokato, MN 55321
Good selection of perennials

The Cummings Garden
22 Robertsville Rd.
Marlboro, NJ 07746
Small and dwarf evergreens, along with companion plants

Daystar
RFD 2
Litchfield, ME 04350
Small shrubs and dwarf conifers

Girard Nurseries
P.O. Box 428
Geneva, OH 44041
Small evergreens, hollies

Greer Gardens
1280 Good Pasture Rd.
Eugene, OR 97401
Rhododendrons, azaleas, and companion plants

Holbrook Farm Nursery
Rte. 2, Box 223B
Fletcher, NC 28732
Selection of new perennials

Klehm Nursery
Rte. 5, Box 197
Penny Rd.
South Barrington, IL 60010
Peonies, iris, hostas and daylilies

Lilypons Water Gardens
6800 Lilypons Rd.
Lilypons, MD 21717
Waterlilies, lotus, and a good selection of aquatic and bog plants

McClure & Zimmerman
108 W. Winnebago, P.O. Box 368
Friesland, WI
Large selection of bulbs

Milaeger's Gardens
4838 Douglas Ave.
Racine, WI 53402
Good selection of perennials

Rocknoll Nursery
9210 U.S. 50
Hillsboro, OH 45133
Rock garden plants, shade plants, and hardy perennials

Roses of Yesterday and Today
Brown's Valley Rd.
Watsonville, CA 95076
Good selection of old garden roses and modern varieties

Shady Oaks Nursery
700 19th Avenue N.E.
Waseca, MN 66093
Plants for shade

John Scheepers, Inc.
Philipsburg Rd., R.D. 2
Middletown, NY 10940
Large selection of bulbs, including lilies

Andre Viette Farm & Nursery
Rte. 1, Box 16
Fisherville, VA 22939
Perennials, daylilies, hostas, iris, and ornamental grasses

Thompson and Morgan
Box 1308
Jackson, NJ 08527
Large selection of flower seeds, also vegetables, bulbs, and other ornamentals

Wayside Gardens
Hodges, SC 29695
Perennials, shrubs, vines, roses, and other ornamentals

White Flower Farm
Litchfield, CT 06759
Good selection of perennials; also roses, shrubs, vines, and bulbs

Gilbert H. W. Wild
Sarcoxie, MO 64862
Peonies and daylilies

Geo. W. Park Seed Co.
Greenwood, SC 29647
Seeds for annuals, vegetables, herbs, and more

The following UK companies which specialize in new flowers, including varieties illustrated in this book, will supply plants direct to North America. Most will send catalogs on written request.

Austin, David
Bowling Green Lane
Albrighton
Wolverhampton
WV7 3HB
(US Agent: Wayside
Gardens, Hodges, SC
29695–0001)
Herbaceous perennials
and roses

Avon Bulbs
Upper Westwood
Bradford-on-Avon
Wilts BA15 2AT
Bulbs, corms, and tubers

Blooms of Bressingham
Bressingham Gardens
Diss
Norfolk IP22 2AB
(US Agent: Wayside
Gardens, Hodges, SC
29695–0001)
Roses, shrubs, and
climbers

**Burncoose and
Southdown Nurseries**
Gwennap
Redruth
Cornwall TR16 6BJ
Roses, shrubs and
climbers

**The John Beach
Clematis Nursery**
9 Grange Gardens
Wellesbourne
Warwicks CV35 9RL

Carcairn Daffodils
Broughshane
Ballymena
Co. Antrim
N. Ireland BT43 7HF
Bulbs, corms, and tubers

John Chambers
15 College Street
Irthlingborough
Wellingborough
Northants NN9 5TU
Wild flowers

**Hilliers Nurseries
(Winchester) Ltd**
Ampfield House
Ampfield
Romsey
Hants SO51 9PA
Roses, shrubs, climbers,
and herbaceous
perennials

Jacques Amand Ltd
The Nurseries
Clamp Hill
Stanmore
Middlesex HA7 3JS
Bulbs, corms, and tubers

Johnson's Seeds
Boston
Lincolnshire PE21 8AD
Annuals, biennials,
bedding plants, and wild
flowers

INDEX

Page numbers in **bold** type refer to flowers depicted in photographs.

ACKNOWLEDGMENTS

PHOTOGRAPHIC CREDITS

b = bottom; c = center; l = left; r = right; t = top

The consultant, author, and publishers gratefully acknowledge the invaluable contribution made by Andrew Lawson who took all the photographs in this book, with the exception of the following:

Title Page: tl Photos Horticultural; tr David Austin Roses; 14 Harry Smith Collection; 15 Photos Horticultural; 32 Eric Crichton; 33 Pat Brindley; 36–37 Harry Smith Collection; 37t Photos Horticultural; 37b Pat Brindley; 38l Pat Brindley; 38 Photos Horticultural; 39 Pat Brindley; 42 A-Z Botanical Collection; 43t Dobies; 43b Harry Smith Collection; 45 Photos Horticultural; 49 Floranova Ltd; 50 Joanne Pavia/The Garden Picture Library; 52 Pat Brindley; 54t Harry Smith Collection; 56–57 Vaugham Fleming/The Garden Picture Library; 58 Harry Smith Collection; 59 Harry Smith Collection; 62 Michael Boys; 63 Photos Horticultural; 69 A-Z Collection; 70 Photos Horticultural; 72t Harry Smith Collection; 76t Photos Horticultural; 76b Pat Brindley; 80, 81t & 82–83 Photos Horticultural; 86–87 & 88t Harry Smith Collection; 88br Rearsby Roses; 89 Photos Horticultural; 90–91 & 92t Harry Smith Collection; 92b Photos Horticultural; 93 Marijke Heuff/ The Garden Picture Library; 94–95 David Austin Roses; 96l Harry Smith Collection; 96br Pat Brindley; 97 Harry Smith Collection; 101b H. C. Meijerink Jr.; 102 Photos Horticultural; 103b Pat Brindley; 106t H. C. Meijerink Jr.; 106b Photos Horticultural; 107 Photos Horticultural; 112l Michael Boys; 112r, 114t, 115 & 116–117 Photos Horticultural; 124t Harry Smith Collection; 124b Eric Crichton; 126–127 Harry Smith Collection; 128t Eric Crichton; 128b Harry Smith Collection; 129 Photos Horticultural; 130l Harry Smith Collection; 131 & 132t Photos Horticultural; 134 Blooms of Bressingham; 135b Eric Crichton; 136 Harry Smith Collection; 137 Photos Horticultural; 138–139 Harry Smith Collection; 140–141 Photos Horticultural; 142bl The Valley Clematis Nursery; 142br & 143 Photos Horticultural; 144 Eric Crichton

Picture on page 142 printed by kind permission of
The Royal Horticultural Society

Artwork pages 146–161 by Norman Bancroft-Hunt

Art Editor Clare Finlaison
Picture Editor Zilda Tandy
Index by Donald Binney

With special thanks to Anne Halpin and Carol Hupping for their contributions to this edition.